Ten Minute Travels

By

Julian Bound

Boats are safe in harbour…
but that's not what boats are made for

Copyright ©JulianBound2022
All rights reserved.
ISBN: 9798839237117

Front cover by Julian Bound
Copyright ©JulianBound2022

Dedication

This book is dedicated to all those met with in close to three decades of travels across Asia, South East Asia and the rest of the world.

Be you friend or foe, lover or rival, know that each one of you had a role to play along my journey, as I hope in some way I did for you. For this I thank you all.

Julian Bound
England, UK
2nd July 2022

Introduction

The following twenty-five stories are taken from countries met with and situations encountered within.

From early travelling days of a visit to America and an invite to Washington's Capital building, to teenage years and a first taste of wanderlust found halfway up Paris' Eiffel Tower, each chapter holds memories of a lifetime spent in travel.

As my travelling years grew so did the distance from a home in England. A nine month journey through Australia, Hawaii, New Zealand, the South Pacific islands of Fiji and The Cook Islands, America and Canada, prompted me to sell all I owned - house, business, car and possessions. All that remained was what I could pack in my backpack as I boarded a plane in Manchester Airport bound for Bangkok.

And so my journey truly began as I walked beneath South East Asian skies for the first time.

Living in Thailand, Cambodia, Indonesia, China, India and Nepal, I learnt to adapt to each country's way of life, finding unique treasures in each place I decided to stop in for a while.

Adventures were found in every new culture happened upon.

Documentary photography became a driving force in my travels across Asia and South East Asia. It was there that I photographed the sulphur miners of Indonesia's Ijen volcano, the police checkpoints in Lhasa, Tibet, the 2015 earthquakes of Nepal, and more.

Another awareness drove my desire to travel. Buddhism.

A first encounter came in the gold and red temples of Northern Thailand and Bangkok. This led to exploring Buddhism and its traditions in Nepal, Bhutan, Cambodia, Myanmar, Tibet, and India, where a meeting with His Holiness the 14th Dalai Lama took place in the town of McLeod Ganj in the foothills of India's far western reaches of the Himalayas.

All these moments encountered within this book are to encourage those who have always longed to travel to do so. To take a step into the unknown. To become all that you can be. To wander, to roam, to travel to places you have always dreamed of. To live in the moment.

Run free, for a little while at least, and believe me when I say, fortune really does favour the bold.

JULIAN BOUND

Contents

Chapter 1	The Hummingbird and The Monk *Chiang Mai, Thailand - 2002*	11
Chapter 2	A First Meal in Kathmandu *Kathmandu, Nepal - 2004*	15
Chapter 3	Sweetcorn and Sharks *Beachcomber Island, Fiji - 2002*	19
Chapter 4	A Meeting With The Dalai Lama *McLeod Ganj, India - 2019*	23
Chapter 5	Croissants and Salvador Dali *Paris, France - 1986*	27
Chapter 6	Pizzas and Starting Blocks *Siem Reap, Cambodia - 2002*	31
Chapter 7	Everest, Lipsticks and Letters *Lhasa, Tibet - 2014*	35
Chapter 8	A Taste of Sulphur *Ijen Volcano, Java, Indonesia - 2015*	39
Chapter 9	A Lunchtime Earthquake *Kathmandu, Nepal - 2015*	43
Chapter 10	Kennedy, Trains and New Freedoms *America – 1976 - 2002*	49
Chapter 11	Kalashnikovs and a Duty of Care *Karen Army Camp, Myanmar - 2005*	53
Chapter 12	Scooters, Scars and Sea Slugs *Rarotonga, The Cook Islands - 2002*	59
Chapter 13	A Copper Canyon Journey *Ciudad Juárez, Mexico - 1996*	63
Chapter 14	Liberty and a First Novel *Hong Kong, China - 2005*	67
Chapter 15	A Portuguese Legacy *Goa, India - 2015*	71

Chapter 16	Monks, Skulls and Monsoons *Siem Reap, Cambodia - 2015*	75
Chapter 17	Yak Butter Tea and a Sacred Lake *Lhasa, Tibet - 2005*	79
Chapter 18	A Walk to The Rose City *Petra, Jordan - 2011*	83
Chapter 19	An Arab Spring, a Taxi and a Sphinx *Cairo, Egypt - 2011*	87
Chapter 20	A Tokyo Respite *Tokyo, Japan - 2016*	91
Chapter 21	Pujas, Mandalas and Fireballs *Sidhbari, India - 2016*	95
Chapter 22	Holy Rites and Luxury Hotels *Paro, Bhutan - 2014*	99
Chapter 23	A First Arrival to a Second Home *Bangkok, Thailand - 2002*	103
Chapter 24	Earthquakes, Stupas and a Sauna *Kathmandu, Nepal - 2016*	107
Chapter 25	Golden Pagodas, Lessons and Slums *Yangon, Myanmar – 2015*	111
Chapter 26	Carpets, Souks and Captains *Tangier, Morocco - 1997*	115
Chapter 27	Taxis, Kites and Ghats *Varanasi, India - 2014*	119
Chapter 28	A Visit to Kyoto and Hiroshima *Kyoto, Japan - 2016*	123
Chapter 29	Cricket, Riots, Buddha and Buses *Colombo, Sri Lanka - 2010*	127
Chapter 30	A Squatter Slum Welcome *Jakarta, Indonesia – 2015*	131
Chapter 31	Maoists, Portraits and Refugees *Pokhara, Nepal – 2014*	135

Chapter 32	The Dalai Lama, Hotels and a Cake *New Delhi, India – 2016*	141
Chapter 33	Chiang Mai: Part I *Chiang Mai, Thailand - 2002*	145
Chapter 34	Chiang Mai: Part II *Chiang Mai, Thailand - 2004*	149
Chapter 35	The Kindness of Strangers *Everywhere*	153

Also by the Author	157
About by the Author	167

Julian Bound

Chapter One

Thailand

The Hummingbird and The Monk

Wat Doi Suthep
Chiang Mai
Thailand
6.30am - 2002

My toes began to warm again.

Riding a scooter feet away from the back of a bus filled to the brim with Chinese tourists, flip flopped feet welcomed the hot exhaust fumes now flowing across them.

It was always a surprise the Asian country I had called home for almost three months had its own share of dawn light chills - sometimes as foreboding as English mornings left behind.

The hilltop temple of Wat Doi Suthep sat another twenty minutes away, its golden stupa and marble flooring reached only by the ascending twisting hillside road now taken.

This was my destination. A want not only to be surrounded by the tranquility of Buddhist concepts new to me, but for the sunrise and inevitable view across Thailand's second biggest city, Chiang Mai.

As the purples of dawn slipped into the blues of a new day sleepy

Chinese tourists were overtaken and left far behind.

A weaving and ever steepening road lay ahead - a road which had taken just six months to complete in the summer of 1935, and so allowing pilgrims to reach their 14th century temple with relative ease.

I shared the road with no-one else; a high pitched scooter engine the only sound echoing through jungle forest on either side of me.

With the temple officially known as 'Wat Phra That Doi Suthep', Doi Suthep is actually the mountain I would traverse twice a week by scooter or red *songthaew* - a small red van carrying shared taxi rides to various destinations.

At 3,520 feet/1,073 metres, Doi Suthep is a Theravada (old school) Buddhist temple. Sacred to the Thai people, many legends swim around its beginnings. One is of a great king who on the back of a white elephant climbed the steep banks of Doi Suthep, at that time called Doi Aoy Chang (Sugar Elephant Mountain) - Doi means mountain in Northern Thai. Nearing the top the elephant came to a stop, trumpeted three times then died. Seen as a favourable omen Wat Phra That Doi Suthep was built on the very spot the elephant came to pass.

The final resting place of a long ago visionary elephant neared, as did Doi Suthep's final bend in the road and a much feared sharp curve - a steep almost forty-five degree turn to the left. A turn I would fall foul of a further six months in the future resulting in two broken toes and a tarmac scuffed elbow and cheekbone.

The scooter whined as it and I fought to climb and turn at the same time. Slowing to almost a halt the road straightened and so came acceleration. A turn of throttle aided my arrival to the temple's dusty tree shaded car park. Opposite the car park Doi Suthep's ornate staircase awaited - its three hundred and nine steps leading devotees and visitors alike up to glistening golden stupa and pagoda.

Flanking the first of temple steps horned Naga dragons rise high.

With piercing glare and gaping jaws of sharp, whiter than white teeth, these Nagas' necks of red and gold scale are held in the mouth of two other dragons. Reproduced in shining tile, each dragon's long green scaled body leads up to the temple, acting as lavish banisters on either side of the steps Doi Suthep's guests must take.

Doi Suthep's monks have another option - a hillside elevator taking them in ease from dusty car park to a temple's marble floor.

The morning's building heat accompanies this visitor's climb. A haste about him in want to catch a Thai sun's break from night. To see dawn fade above a now much loved city, and home.

Only a few others climb these steps this morning. Those buses of Chinese tourists are still yet to arrive. No doubt an infamous steep bend in the road is playing a part in their lack of appearance.

Several followers of The Buddha leave Doi Suthep's final step and make toward golden shrines. Between hands held in prayer each carries candles, three incense sticks and a white tulip bud on a long green stem. All are keen to present their gifts as blessings.

I follow those eager to give prayer then glance back from the dizzying height of the temple's last step. There is still no sign of other foreigners such as I.

Leaving behind a summit climbed sees entrance into temple grounds. I am welcomed by a statute of its white elephant forefather. White painted trunk, legs and hide are straddled by red straps holding a saddle in place. There a small golden stupa sits atop a blue cushion.

The morning's slight breeze ignites a soft tinkling of metal. Small wafer-thin hearts hang from the eaves of shrines surrounding the temple complex. Signifying a donation given from temple guests, each fine bronze blessings is inscribed with the name of a loved one now passed.

A leaving of footwear on designated shelving and a barefoot step into Doi Suthep's main arena.

Large metal cast bells hang at head height. Line upon line of them border the place those have come to bless and be blessed. To the right a huge brass gong stands, its dimpled centre ready to be struck by the side of a devotee's clenched fist.

Amid all these bells, gongs and shrines stands the stupa - home to a fragment of bone from Lord Buddha himself. At twenty-four metres high, the stupa's golden tiles begin to shine in dawn's continued break.

Soon a Northern Thai sun will rise, allowing the stupa's golden tiers to warm those who circle its four walls; three times clockwise in devotion, three smouldering incense sticks and a long stemmed tulip bud held between palms pressed together.

Of these sights I will see later. For now a sunrise beckons.

A bench is found and a sunrise is received. Chiang Mai below is bathed in orange rays and the River Ping glistens on its meander southwards to Bangkok's Chao Phraya River, and beyond.

A silhouette blocks my view. Short in stature, the monk's orange robes are a reminder that I am a guest in another's home.

"Hello," he says to me. "My name is Tu Long Bin." He pauses and smiles. "But not like Bin Laden."

Still sharp in people' minds, Bin Laden's acts on New York had taken place only a year ago. Taken by surprise I return a smile.

"You like coffee?" I am asked.

"Yes," comes my reply.

Hesitant at first, I follow the monk I would come to know as Tu Long. Leading me away from a glimmering stupa we step down stone steps beneath a green canopy sparkling in morning sun. I follow into a cabin perched on Doi Suthep's hillside.

A small corridor leads to an open balcony. Looking out onto Chiang Mai's rooftops far in the distance, clouds pass by close enough to touch. At times a stray tendril causes a momentary chill to flow across this monk's home.

Coffee is prepared, a cigarette is shared.

So comes a lesson in meditation. Talked through a breathing technique we close our eyes. After a few moments mine open.

I look once more to the clouds, unaware that this will not be my only visit to this balcony. Unaware that my host and I will be writing and narrating Doi Suthep's dictaphone guide, one which tourists will listen to for many years to come. Unaware that I will be given a *monk pass* allowing me to use an elevator to the temple instead of climbing three-hundred and nine steps between two dragons' green scales. Unaware that in six months' time, broken toes and a scuffed elbow and cheekbone would come from racing to an appointment in Chiang Mai's centre after a morning reciting a visitor's guide.

I close my eyes once more. I try to carry out what has been taught.

My eyes open again. I look to my right.

A hummingbird hovers just above a balcony rail. Fine green feathers shine and glisten as minute adjustments are made in the humming bird's stance.

Then it is gone.

I turn back to the monk before me.

Eyes open, Tu Long smiles.

Chapter Two

NEPAL

A First Meal in Kathmandu

Thamel
Kathmandu
Nepal
5.30pm - 2004

Backpack straps cut into tired shoulders, yet this feels like home. A oneness within the self. Hungry to confront unknown adventures sure to lay ahead. Leaving Kathmandu airport's small red brick walls that step into the unknown is greeted by taxi drivers' calls.

So arrives a game of bartering, frowns and eventual smiles.

A driver is chosen. A trusty backpack is thrown onto the back seat of my small white Fiat ride. I opt to sit up front.

With the offer of a cigarette and acceptance, we drive into a Nepalese dusk highlighted by two glowing tips of Thai Marlboro Lights. Our destination? - Kathmandu's centre, and a promised room in a hotel belonging to my driver's *brother*.

A radio filled with female Bollywood singers accompanies our drive through ever darkening streets, an apt accompaniment for new sights now seen, the evening's cool touch so different to a Thai climate left far behind.

As we drive I watch people wrapped in warm blankets gather around street side mobile kitchens. Plumes of silver steam rise above the crowds as vendors offer dishes of dhal curries and hot momo dumplings, delicacies as yet to be tasted.

The streets are left behind as the driver beside me navigates through narrowing lanes lined with small doors. Fleetingly highlighted in a taxi's strong beam, each door is painted a different colour of red, blue, yellow, orange or green.

With the lane getting impossibly tight the taxi escapes at the last moment into a vast courtyard. Three tall buildings are lit by moonlight. My driver nods to one and pulls up beside it. Greeted by the *brother* and with all concerned paid I am guided to my room.

The ensuing staircase causes another bite from backpack straps across my shoulders. I feel the weight of all I own in the world packed tight within the bulging pack on my back. I also feel light.

There is a true lightness within the freedom of having little possessions. A concept so clear to me now. A perception only discovered after years already spent living on the road. Each item within my bag was there for a reason. For why carry something on your back if it serves no purpose?

The hotel owner disappears as I enter my home for the night. With backpack thrown onto one of the two beds in the room a toiletry bag is placed in the bathroom - an act to confirm I am home.

A TV sits in one corner. After warming up it at last provides a channel filled with Hollywood movies. A treat for later. For now a shower and change is in order… Then an evening in exploration of a capital and country never visited before.

Showered and dressed the tourist area of Thamel is my chosen destination. It seems Nepal's night sky commences its march into full darkness between the hours of 6.30pm and 7pm, much the same as all other countries met with throughout South East Asia.

This is my first day after leaving Thailand and eighteen months of living there. Nepal will be a home now. As will other countries to follow. Home is now marked by wherever I place my bag down in this, the nomadic part of my life.

Chiang Mai's jungle city seems far from me now, as do those Thai sunsets that disappear in haste - only to be replaced with dark starlit skies within the blink of an eye.

I walk through dimly lit streets and alleyways. It feels strange to be wearing a jacket in early evening again.

A year and a half of humid Thai nights gave rise to t-shirt or light collared shirt, not the jacket I pull tight around me now.

The lights and noise of motorbikes and cars with continual beeping horns guide my way. An excitement present. A want to see the new. To see how others live in the shadow of the world's highest mountain range.

After twenty minutes I step onto Thamel's dusty streets. Hunger sets in. The food Nepal offers causes a further distance from Thailand within me. Curries of green and red, chicken and cashew nut dishes and fresh pineapple on a stick are all absent. Plates of dhal, rice and chicken on the bone sit beside white steamed dumplings, each plump package sitting in a bamboo slat tray.

Walking by shops filled with cashmere blankets and silk scarves I see a sign which will release me from my hunger. In tall hand painted yellow letters it says Cheese Sandwich.

Part of me berates myself for not trying the foreign delicacies around me, but the idea of a cheese sandwich wins through.

I step into the small shop. A large counter runs from front door to rear of the shop.

Behind the counter a man stands up and smiles. A young boy sits on the floor behind him. Guessing the boy to be four years old, he sits engrossed in the toy he plays with. I feel sorry for the boy. I see his favoured toy is a simple block of wood, its brown edges just big enough to be held in such small hands.

"Namaste," the man says.

"Cheese sandwich please, sir," I reply.

The man reaches behind the counter and produces two slices of bread. Soon buttered and with a single lettuce leaf positioned on one the man looks back to his son.

Leaning down he takes the block of wood from the child and places it next to my half made sandwich.

The child's cries fill the shop as his father starts to slice what I now realise is not a block of wood, but a block of cheese.

I say nothing as the sandwich is completed. Pushed down by a large palm my dinner is wrapped in a sheet of newspaper.

The child's cries come to an abrupt stop as his father hands him back his favourite toy - it's one bright yellow side soon to disappear under the constant turning of an infant's fingers.

I thank the man and step back onto Kathmandu's streets. Tired and ready for bed I make back to my hotel, two slices of discarded cheese in my wake.

The twenty minutes it took to arrive to Thamel seem longer as I crisscross street after street and alleyway after alleyway. Soon an hour passes with still no sign of the moonlit hotel I had been delivered to.

Another hour passes. I am no closer to where my entire belongings in the world sit, packed away in a backpack in front of the TV set that promised me a movie on my return.

In another eleven years I would come to know Kathmandu's streets well. Nepal's capital would become my home for close to four years when working as a documentary photographer for the United Nations and various disaster charities, both during and after the country's devastating earthquakes of 2015.

Those moments remained far in the future as the hunt for my hotel continued. A future that would see to using digital photography, not the film camera I had tucked away in a yet to be found hotel.

It would take a further thirty minutes to find my hotel. Relief overruled any hunger still felt.

Beneath an itchy hotel blanket the TV observed its promise – the movie? *Vertical Limit*, a mountaineering story set in part within the Himalayas, the same mountain range that would watch over my first night's sleep in Nepal.

Chapter Three

Fiji

Sweetcorn and Sharks

Beachcomber Island
Fiji
2002

The plan had been to visit all of Fiji's islands. I arrived at the first and stayed.

An hour or so boat ride from the main Fijian island of Viti Levu, Beachcomber Island is the first of the Mamanuca Islands. Arcing northwards through the South Pacific Ocean, these small islands run parallel with Viti Levu's western coastline.

A plan to island hop from one paradise to another seemed futile on stepping onto Beachcomber Islands warm sands. I had found my Eden. I was to stay for a sun kissed eighteen days.

A supposed three month trip exploring Australia would eventually evolve into a nine month journey around the world.

Unknown to me then, Fiji would mark the near middle of my trip, with the Cook Islands, America and Canada yet to come. These destinations were decided by the flip of a coin…

Owning a busy business back home in England, I knew I had to return. My heart felt otherwise. This new found freedom of little if any responsibility gave a much needed replenishment to a once jaded soul. A renewal of self. Enhanced by friendships made whilst on the road - no matter how brief those kinships were.

A coin seemed the only way to show me where to go next, my destination left to fate. If the coin landed heads I would go to my next chosen country to visit, whereas if landing tails this would mean the game was up and it was time to fly home to the UK.

Choosing heads each time, a first coin flip in Hawaii had seen to my arrival in Fiji, via a two day return to Australia and a twenty-three hour layover in Auckland, New Zealand. Upon the sands of Beachcomber Island, another coin toss would land heads and I would head for The Cook Islands. From there a flight to Los Angeles was denoted by another coin landing heads, as was a flight to Vancouver where another island was visited, resulting in an afternoon of drinking, of which my drinking partner and I got matching tattoos - my first, the next being in China on my thirty-sixth birthday four years in the future.

An eventual flip of tails one week after that first tattoo would result in a plane ticket bought the next day and a return to England.

But, for now, I was on Beachcomber Island.

Also known as *Tai*, and *barefoot island* - it is commonplace not to wear shoes on the island, Beachcomber Island became popular with tourists in the 1960's. Its legacy has continued as now it is regarded as the party island to visit if in the South Pacific.

Surrounded by warm crystal clear waters, the island's beach is just over half a kilometer in circumference – it took an average of twenty minutes to circumnavigate the whole island.

To the south of the island there is an open air bar with a sand dune dancefloor. In the middle of the island a wall less dormitory houses over one hundred bunkbeds within. Below each bunkbed are two locked boxes with keys, one for each bunkbed occupant. The key has the number of the bunk on it and dangles on a piece of string to be hung around the neck. This was how you paid for everything on the island. Your number was taken when you bought something, which was then added to a bill you would pay when leaving the island. This practice did not work for everyone.

On one occasion whilst in the island's reception room, I watched one backpacker physically shake when given their bill for a week of partying. My reason for being in that reception that day was a medical one.

The island's nurse counted fifty-two angry swollen mosquito bites across my back and arms.

"You have too much potassium in you, Mr. Julian," she said, calling me by the name she would throughout my stay. "The mosquitos like the way you taste," she giggled.

I understood her diagnosis. On first arriving in Australia I fell ill and was told I was low on potassium. So for the next four months until my arrival to Beachcomber Island, I had eaten two bananas a day. Much to the delight of Fiji's hungry mosquitos.

A change from an open dormitory bunkbed and to a single private room solved the problem. Now I was just a few steps from the large open air dining area I would meet new found friends each morning for breakfast.

It was easy to meet others on the island. There wasn't much else to do but swim, sunbathe, or if energetic enough play volley ball or tag rugby with the locals, two of which were ex-Fijian international players. It would be one breakfast time that I suggested another game to play to my tablemates.

"Look," I said. "We can fill an empty water bottle with food then go feed the fish."

This is what we did. Sweetcorn was the easiest food to fill the bottle with and there was an abundance of it..

With bottles filled to the brim we fed the fish that swam at a small coral reef ten metres from Beachcomber's southwestern tip - a tall red and white striped pole poked out of the water to mark its spot.

Each day bigger fish came, not so much for the sweetcorn, but for the smaller fish who devoured what we provided. By the fourth day the novelty had worn off and we were onto other things, also the fish were getting a little bit too big to be around.

A few days later laying on the beach two young women deep in conversation walked by.

"They said," the one said.

"Who?" The other asked.

"In reception, they said they had never seen it before." Both girls looked to the island's southwestern tip. "They said it's the first time sharks have been spotted so close to the beach."

My sunburnt cheeks paled. I knew the reason for the appearance of sharks on Beachcomber's coastline. There was no denying an increase of fish both in quantity and size searching for provided sweetcorn had led to the arrival of Tiger, Silver and Blacktip sharks. A menacing arrival only metres away from where I lay.

It would not be until the next day when I found out talk of nearing sharks was true.

I had been in the sea before hearing talk of sharks.

Days earlier as a scorching sun took hold I had ventured into the water. Swimming from the beach two black eyes popped out of the ocean before me. Thinking it was a seal I swam closer. I stopped. It wasn't a seal (I'm not sure there are any in the South Pacific) it was a black jellyfish floating on the surface. I needn't worry, there was no sting about them. It was the same breed of black jellyfish the local children would wear on their heads as hats to entertain the tourists.

The day after eavesdropping on two young women talking of sharks a friend asked if I would join them snorkeling. I agreed, thinking there would be safety in numbers.

With the sun burning across shoulders and back we both swam forwards immersed in a display of angel fish below.

Continuing onwards the water took on a cool chill. I felt a jab in my ribs. Looking to my snorkeling partner, the finger she had poked me with was now pointing ahead of us.

Two long dark shadows floated in and out of vision. One moved closer giving us a sharper view. Then I saw its eye. Dark and lifeless above a mouthful of a sharp untidy teeth, the Tiger shark watched us intently.

I looked to how far from the island we were. The ten metre pole from the beach was a good twenty metres away.

With not another look to sharks encountered, we glanced to one another then began to swim as fast as we could.

Reaching the shoreline I thought of an old Tom and Jerry cartoon where in a similar situation, Tom had left the water and continued to swim in the sand far up the beach.

On reaching the safety of Beachcomber's shores I wasn't far off that cartoon cat.

Chapter Four

India

A Meeting With The Dalai Lama

Temple Road
McLeod Ganj
India
7.00am - 2019

Red prayers wheels of gold embossed lettering turn in seeming perpetual motion. The hand of a Buddhist monk, nun, devotee or tourist aids an almost continual spin. These are Temple Road's blessings for Siddhartha Gautama, the one who became The Buddha.

I have walked this road on and off for close to two decades. Each time I have passed by these street side wheels laden with prayers, spinning endlessly in a row on a temple's outer walls. Familiar this may be. This is not my reason for being here.

My walk down Temple Road's downward slope continues until another road is met. Much steeper, The Dalai Lama Temple sits at its end. At last I see the gated entrance to McLeod's yellow temple. In less than one hour I will meet His Holiness the 14th Dalai Lama in those temple's grounds.

McLeod Ganj has always drawn me to it.

A sheer uphill fifteen minute drive from the town of Dharamsala, the small town of McLeod Ganj sits in the foothills of India's far western edges of the Himalaya Mountain range. It has been home to the present Dalai Lama since 1959, when first arriving in India after escaping Tibet. His Holiness began a life of exile from that moment in the upper reaches of India's northern state Praha Ganj.

Since the Dalai Lama's arrival to India over eighty thousand Tibetans have followed His path. Each escaping Chinese rule in their homelands to find a safer home on MacLeod Ganj's hillsides.

I have encountered His Holiness on two other occasions.

The first was in the September of 2014 in the temple I now walk towards some five years later, when with the aid of a press pass gained after a visit to The Tibetan Parliament in Exile (found half way down McLeod's steep single road to Dharamsala), I was allowed to enter The Dalai Lama Temple with my camera and join the Indian media in their press box. This was the first time I photographed His Holiness. The second was in a very different setting.

In 2016 the Oberoi Hotel in New Delhi held a party for the 14th Dalai Lama in honour of His Holiness reaching his eightieth birthday. The event was for only one hundred and fifty of His Holiness' closest friends and confidents. In a most auspicious way I was allowed into the celebration and took my second set of photos.

There would be no camera today (His Holiness' own photographer would provide wanted photos of visitors standing beside His Holiness), all I had was my invite and the book planned to present to the Dalai Lama himself.

Only one week earlier I had been in the UK. After close to a year travelling through Malaysia, Cambodia and Thailand, my arrival back to England was in sharp contrast to the humidity and searing sun of Asia. It was now the end of November and the onset of Christmas ran evident throughout my hometown's streets and shops strewn with tinsel.

A ticket was bought for India with a return which would see me back in Manchester Airport two days before Christmas Day. I had four weeks to embrace India. I also had two plans.

With one plan to walk the streets and Ghats of Varanasi once more as done so five years earlier, my other plan was to return to McLeod Ganj with two assignments – one, to give the Dalai Lama a photography book I had authored of a journey undertaken when travelling through seven Buddhist countries in seven months, the other was to visit the mediation teachers first encountered fourteen years earlier and visited many times since.

However, there was one thing which may have hampered my plans.

I didn't know if the Dalai Lama or my meditation teachers were in McLeod Ganj. Leaving Manchester Airport one rainy November evening I was in fate's hands - leaving it to chance that those I planned to meet with would be there.

After two nights in Delhi I landed in Dharamsala's small airport. With a taxi ride to McLeod's centre I took a room in a favoured hotel – the same room I have always stayed in when in McLeod Ganj – its high balcony overlooking steep valley sides of bright coloured rooftops, homes to second, third and further generations of Tibetan refugee.

Fate proved on my side. Fortune truly does favour the bold.

My meditation teachers were home. Due to leave for a warmer climate that morning they held back on their travels. A strong intuition telling them an old student was to arrive that day.

Fortune continued to shine as I discovered a good friend of many years was also in McLeod, both of us sharing an affinity rarely found outside the nomadic lifestyle at times kept.

With one plan seen to fruition and in the company of my friend again another plan came to light. The Dalai Lama was home too.

After another visit to the Tibetan Parliament in Exile I was given an invite to meet His Holiness. Our meeting was to take place in the Dalai Lama Temple grounds at 7.30am, in two days' time.

Those two days ran swift and I soon found myself walking down an ever descending road at 7am, the entrance to The Dalai Lama Temple getting closer with every footstep.

After rigorous security checks where phones, money, keys and whatever else was in your pockets were put in a tray to be collected later, my book was placed with other attendee's gifts for His Holiness to receive later.

Directed up a slight hill I joined the many others ready to meet the Dalai Lama. Tibetans took the front of the queue, next were the Indians, and then me. Behind were two other Europeans. Behind them stood a group of twenty French Buddhists.

The Dalai Lama appeared and the queue began to move forward.

A Tibetan official began to group people together.

Assembled with the two Europeans behind me we chatted and smiled, nerves taking place on shuffling ever closer to His Holiness.

Those meeting the Dalai Lama ahead received a scarf blessing which was then placed around their neck, they then had a brief chat and moved on. Our group of three's meeting would be much different.

As each of us stepped forward two of our party were ushered to sit at His Holiness' right hand side. I was placed standing to His Holiness' left. Taking my hand in his, the Dalai Lama reached out his right and held hands with those sitting at his side. Then he began to speak.

The French Buddhists formed a semi-circle in front of His Holiness as he spoke of the world's need for peace and compassion.

Halfway through the Dalai Lama's twenty minute talk I looked to His Holiness beside me. It dawned on me what was happening – I was standing next to The Dalai Lama, my hand in his.

The Dalai Lama continued to speak and without a beat rubbed his thumb across the back of my hand in reassurance – sure as I am, he had sensed my realisation of the situation I now found myself.

With His Holiness' talk complete he gave a nod and smile to each of those whose hand had been in his.

Myself and the two Europeans were then ushered away to the sound of His Holiness the 14th Dalai Lama blessing the group of French Buddhists who had waited so patiently to meet him.

Chapter Five

France

Croissants and Salvador Dali

The Eiffel Tower
Paris
France
1986

"I'm halfway up the Eiffel Tower, Gran. Don't tell me Mum."

After climbing a metal staircase and finding a pay phone in the Eiffel Tower's first floor restaurant, these were the lunchtime words my recipient in England heard her sixteen year old grandson say. Now there was at least one person who knew where I was.

Telling my parents of the local weekend party I was going to until Sunday night, I instead stood in a travel agents one Friday morning.

"I want to go to Paris," I said to a travel agent's bemused looks.

I bought a return ticket to Paris with the proceeds of what I sold days before. A shirt, and the golf clubs I had become disenchanted with.

Boarding a 10am train to London, then another to Dover, a ferry was then taken. It would not be until half way across the English Channel heading for Calais that my weekend really began.

I can't remember if I approached them or they me, but anyway, we all sat together as our ferry pitched and tossed on strong autumnal seas.

Although two years older than me, the three of us enjoyed one another's company; they two teenage girls on their way to meet boyfriends in Paris.

Arriving in Calais, The Orient Express stood on the platform opposite, only adding to a young mind's sense of adventure. We took a train to central Paris together, sharing a carriage and a couple of bottles of sweet tasting red and blue label Thunderbird wine.

Drinking and laughter ensued. That laughter quieted on our 1am arrival to Paris' Gare du Nord station where two boyfriends glowered, unimpressed by the extra party their girlfriends now laughed with.

The two boyfriends warmed as I told them I didn't have a clue where I was staying (I was sixteen, I hadn't thought that far ahead).

Given instructions to where I could find a cheap room, a phone number was given to me written on paper torn from a cigarette packet. I was to ring if I wanted to join them for a Saturday night trawling through Paris' bars and clubs.

Saying my farewells and with a phone number safe in my pocket I made for St. Lazare station and the suggested hotels running along the street beside it.

As told the street was lined with places to stay. Watching a couple walk into one I followed. In the lobby there were more couples. I decided this must be a safe hotel - one for families.

A grunt from the receptionist prompted me to step forward. I asked how much a room was.

"For the hour, or the night?" The string vested receptionist said in a thick Parisian accent. I laughed, still under the effect of a train's drinking session.

"For the night," I replied, my smile fading to the glare received.

Handing over the French franc equivalent of twelve English pounds I took the key thrust at me and found my room. Sleep came fast, cocooned as I was in what was more a hammock than a bed.

The next morning I paid for another night in the hotel, realising at last that the hotel was not for families as so thought on my arrival.

Now Paris was mine to discover.

Buying a carnet of ten metro tickets saw me travelling in all directions. Once the Paris underground system was conquered and understood I made my way to The Eiffel Tower.

With little spare money for the easier option of an elevator, I instead paid a minimal fee and began to climb a staircase within one of the tower's legs. A metallic clang sounded out with each arduous footstep before I reached the first floor and searched for a phone.

After telling my gran where I was and of the adventure I was having I headed northwards to the holy Sacré-Coeur Basilica.

On Sacré-Coeur's white marble church steps I ate two warm croissants bought earlier from a Pigalle patisserie, my view resting on a tower just left far in the distance.

Walking to the side of my Catholic church lunch place I followed lanes of cobbled stone into the heart of Montmartre - once home to Picasso and art's usual suspects of Miro and Manet, Toulouse-Lautrec, Renoir and Van Gogh. There was another famous artist present. On a back street I stumbled on a Salvador Dali gallery.

There were original drawing for sale. Dali was still alive in 1986 and a small original, signed sketch could be bought for £70.

I had the money on me. I looked to notes in my hand and then to a wanted drawing. Putting my money back in my jeans pocket I looked to a phone number given to me at 1am in Gare du Nord train station.

Not having enough money for a drawing and a night out, I left Dali's pencil masterpieces and returned to my hotel, eager for the night to begin.

Deciphering how to use a French pay phone and contact those met with on the ferry, I also managed to find the small bar told of.

The two girls on the ferry and their boyfriends brought three others with them. Together we spent the night drinking in Parisian bars and clubs.

At 5am the next morning I left the small flat we had all returned to after the bars had closed, and took a metro from Paris' southern suburbs and to the St Lazare hotel room I had paid for but not used. I had a couple of francs to my name and a return ticket home.

Returning to Montmartre's Sacré-Coeur after checking out of my hotel I sat on church steps once more.

Watching early morning street cleaners brush their long green brooms over cobble stones I ate one final croissant bought with the last of my money.

That Sunday as I travelled by train, ferry, train and train again, my thoughts were not on the Dali drawing I had forfeited for my Saturday night out. I had discovered something I have always tried to recapture in my travels far and wide ever since.

Whilst climbing those Eiffel Tower steps I had paused as an October breeze brushed my cheeks.

Looking out over Paris streets bustling beneath a blue cloudless sky, an immense sense of freedom had arrived to me. A liberty that could have carried me to the top of the tower I now climbed.

This is why I think I have always travelled. To recapture a feeling met with that day on the Eiffel Tower's rust coloured steps – freedom's touch teasing an already awakening wanderlust.

On some occasions I have met with a similar sense of such freedom, yet never has it been as strong as that day on that Eiffel Tower staircase. A moment which changed my life's course, and worth more than all the Dali's in the world.

Chapter Six

Cambodia

Pizzas and Starting blocks

Siem Reap
Cambodia
2002

I woke to my head bouncing off a mini bus window.

Sitting up, the eyes of other backpackers were on me. On hitting another deep pothole like the one which had woken me, I asked my three travelling companions how long the road had been like this.

"For the last two hours," I was told.

I pieced everything together as our ride swerved unsuccessfully to avoid another hole in the road – the unkempt highway carrying us to Cambodia's northern city of Siem Reap, a further six hours away.

I remembered the border crossing from Thailand into Cambodia, as did I seeing my passport stamped and given back to me. The rest was a blank.

The three travelling companions I had travelled with for the last month in Bangkok, Phuket, the Thai islands of Kho Samui and Koh Phangan for a full moon party and now Cambodia, explained all to me.

Worried I would not sleep on the mini bus from the Cambodian border one of our gang gave me a small blue pill. He said it would help me sleep.

Swallowing that small blue pill when alighting the bus delivering us to the Thai/Cambodian border, my friend asked for the other half of the pill he had just given me. It was too late I had taken all of it. My first ever dose of valium. All ten milligrams of it.

I was told I had collapsed after being stamped into Cambodia, then carried to our minibus waiting to take us to Siem Reap - on which I awoke two hours later.

Siem Reap itself proved another world. A world which travellers seek. A place differing from what our western homes offer.

With only a handful of hotels and streets of orange dust, Cambodia's second biggest city gave that feeling of being somewhere new. Somewhere never experienced before. Everything, a beer, cigarettes or a plates of french-fries cost one American dollar, a currency most craved for by the Cambodians.

This Siem Reap of 2002 would become unrecognisable in only fifteen years' time.

Where once there were only two bars, in a decade and a half the streets they sat on would become Pub Street. Lined with bars and restaurants, Siem Reap's centre would become a mecca for backpackers from across the world to enjoy a night of cheap beer, liquor and snacks of deep fried tarantula, scorpion, grasshopper or a small snake on a stick.

Although the changes to Siem Reap through time are so immense, the city still holds its charm and sense of fun.

It is easy to reminisce and say what a pity it is that places visited twenty years ago have lost their charm. – 'they used to wash my laundry in the river, beating my washing across a rock to get clean, those days are gone, now they've got washing machines.'

And so they should, how selfish is it to want countries visited years ago to stay the same - their population to remain in poverty and forego the basic items we in the west have in abundance.

Siem Reap became a constant in my travels through Asia for over twenty years. As with many other cities and towns across South East Asia, I would watch Siem Reap grow and change. I would roll through those changes with no reminiscences at all - Its ok to look back on your life, just don't stare.

With Siem Reap's Angkor Wat temple complex seen and a city's French colonial lanes and avenues walked, a visit to the city outskirts and the war museum there would see to a first photograph to appear on the BBC News - taken of our guide, Sinnat, sitting with his false leg standing up beside him (the result of standing on not one but two landmines).

Returning to Siem Reap seventeen years later in 2019, I found our old guide Sinnat and showed him the photo of his younger self which was published for all the world to see.

Leaving Siem Reap a six hour boat ride southwards through the country saw us four travellers enter the Mekong Delta and land at the harbour of Cambodia's capital, Phnom Penh.

Visiting grounds of Cambodia's recent genocidal past, the city's S21 Prison and the Killing Fields, understanding came of how little if any infrastructure there was within the country. It appeared Pol Pot's legacy had continued over a decade after his philosophy of year zero.

City centre bars hosted our evenings, one patron of which I would meet by chance a year to the day later, although that is another story in itself. It would be that night on returning to the guesthouse on the edge of an inner city lake that would confirm choices made only two months earlier.

The wanderlust first stirred in a sixteen year old's eventful trip to Paris had risen within my thirty year old self.

The busy Barber Shop I owned and of which I employed several, no longer gave me joy. A journey around the world (the one where Fiji's sharks and mosquitos had taken a liking to me) had changed my way of thinking. I sold everything I owned – the business, the house, the furniture, the car, until all I owned was a backpack full of clothes, and a one way flight ticket to Bangkok.

One night after returning from Phnom Penh's bars I climbed the staircase leading to the guesthouse rooftop.

Alone, but for a packet of Marlboro Lights and a lighter, I looked to my view over the city. Dawn was about to break and under a blue hazy sky a nearby mosque began its call to prayer. It was in this moment, so far removed from having a shop and the responsibility of being a home owner, I knew my decision to leave all I knew behind was the right one to have made.

The next morning after my epiphany on the rooftop of a Phnom Penh guesthouse, the four of us prepared to leave for the seafront town of Sihanouville, a five hour bus ride north along Cambodia's western coastline, a beachfront which was then forbidden to walk on due to landmines.

Wanting to get food for our trip we came across Phnom Penh's famous Happy Pizza shop. We got an extra-large - with extra *happy* toppings.

Boarding a bus we each eat a slice and waited for its effects. After thirty minutes the results of any high were minimal. Choosing to have another piece we discovered one of our party sat at the back of the bus had eaten the lot.

"I was hungry," he told us, the remnants of tomato, cheese and a special green herb on his chin.

This resulted in our group of four becoming three the next day. Our hungry culprit was confined to bed, still very much under the influence of those *happy* toppings.

A horrendous boat ride on turbulent seas and a short bus ride minus any pizzas was taken to the Cambodian/Thai border town of Poipet. Missing the border closing time by five minutes one more night was spent under a Cambodian moon.

An arrival back into the arms of Bangkok came with a surprise. Other travellers met with on our journey through Thai islands and Cambodia were in Bangkok also.

It was night to remember as within a few weeks we would all part ways. Yet our time together proved a valuable starting block to begin our journeys alone, and maybe find ourselves somewhere along the way.

This tale written here of Cambodia is not so much a telling of events, but of expressing the bonds of friendship at times found when on the road. Kinships often evolving in but moments.

I am sure we all had our reasons to visit the other side of the world and forget what had been left behind. It was those reasons which escaped us for those few months.

An allowance to breath and to live for the moment, moments which were filled with laughter every day. This is what those friendships gave.

A camaraderie rarely touched upon again.

Chapter Seven

Tibet

Everest, Lipsticks and Letters

Lhasa
Tibet
6pm - 2014

The Tibetan night drew in with a high altitude sunset blazing orange and red.

This was my second time in Tibet. Lhasa's streets had been walked nine years previous, almost to the week. The Tibetan capital was unrecognizable now. Four lane highways stretched in and out of the city where a couple of roads once made do.

One place remained the same back then. The Tibetan quarter the Chinese government *allowed* the Tibetans to keep as it had for centuries. This Tibetan stronghold within the grounds of Barkhor Square was one of the reasons I was here.

A few months earlier when in the Tibetan Parliament in Exile getting a pass to photograph the Dalai Lama, His Holiness' press officer asked of my travel plans. Telling him of Nepal and Bhutan, he had sat upright when hearing of an intended visit to Tibet.

"Would you do something for us when you are there?" He asked.

He told how Lhasa's area of Barkhor Square and its homes and shops allowed to remain Tibetan were under threat.

The Chinese government had broken their assurances that Lhasa's Tibetan quarter would have no Chinese influence. Now Chinese hotels were being built on once promised land.

I was asked by the Tibetan government if I would take photos of the construction of these Chinese hotels.

I agreed to do so.

There was another reason why I was walking Lhasa's street once more. A Tibetan refugee met with in India asked if I would deliver letters to their cousin in Lhasa. Agreeing to do so I hid the letters in my backpack - and the lipstick I had been given to deliver also. It seems Lhasa doesn't have this particular shade.

Arriving in Nepal with my photography mission, a bundle of letters and a lipstick, I booked a place on a bus of twelve tourists for a tour from Kathmandu and into the heart of Lhasa.

Beginning in Kathmandu our journey north would see us cross the Nepal/Tibetan border and travel through the towns and cities of Tingri, Gyantse and Shigatse. It would be seven days until reaching Lhasa for a three day stay before flying back to Kathmandu.

The group jelled well. Argentinians, Swedish, Danish and the Dutch all spoke English, myself the only English person on the bus.

At the Nepal/Tibetan border we were ushered onto the Friendship Bridge to carry us over the Sun Kosi River and into Tibet. Our Nepalese guide approached. He pointed to my camera bag.

"What is in there?" He asked.

As well as my backpack filled with all my worldly belongings I carried my camera bag over one shoulder. Opening it I showed my camera equipment and laptop. The guide shook his head.

"They will not let you in the country with this," he told me. "Give me your laptop."

Putting my laptop in a plastic carrier bag he walked across the bridge to our Tibetan guide waiting to take us to Lhasa.

I was last to reach the security point to get stamped into Tibet. The young uniformed Chinese woman looked from my passport to me three times before calling her superior who repeated her actions.

With the Tibetan border just feet away, the contraband letters and lipstick hidden in my backpack began to weigh heavy on me.

The rest of our group, our Tibetan tour guide and the Nepalese guide holding my laptop in a plastic bag stared back, wondering what this English man was doing, or had done.

After a very long twenty minutes I was allowed into Tibet with a nod and insincere smile off a superior immigration officer.

The journey north through Tibet was both beautiful and arduous. Accommodation equaled sleeping in clothes most freezing high altitude nights, this was November. This was what added to the adventure, as did a breakfast of one egg and a slab of heavy Tibetan bread - maybe noodles if in luck.

At 7am on the third day we were told we would be visiting Mount Everest's first basecamp. A surprise to us all, I pulled my $10 fake North Face jacket close to me. I looked to the others. Almost all were unprepared for what was to come. I spotted two denim jackets as an only defense in the foothills of the world's highest mountain. There would be only two who suffered.

With Mount Everest standing at 29,029 feet/8,848 metres, Tibet's first base camp stands at an altitude of 16,900 feet/5,150 metres. First base camp is for Sherpa and climbers to acclimatise in often minus sixteen degree temperatures before ascending Everest's northeastern ridge.

It has been known for some climbers to scale Everest on the Nepal side then descend on the Tibetan side only to be met by Chinese immigration. I don't know what they say to those climbers, but I wouldn't be surprised if the Chinese didn't send them back up.

There would be no ascending anything for me that day. Arriving at base camp I delved into the world of altitude sickness.

Listless and not knowing what to do with myself I counted myself lucky as I watched another of our party suffer. Taking off his denim jacket he revealed arms of deep blue from elbows to fingertips.

Feeling a bit left out for not being given oxygen as was my blue armed friend, I returned to the bus longing to be just a few hundred feet nearer sea level. An eventual return to lower altitudes solved an aching head, limbs and nausea - as did it another's once blue arms.

Halfway through our trip we visited Shigatse's Buddhist monastery of Tashilhunpo. We were told up to two thousand burgundy robed monks once lived within Tashilhunpo. Due to China's desire to destroy Tibetan culture, Tashilhunpo's monastery grounds were now home to less than two hundred monks.

China's want to absorb Tibet into the Chinese mainland has been shown in many ways - from offering Chinese citizens the chance to avoid paying taxes if they move to Tibet and set up business there, to infiltrating Lhasa's nightclubs and bars with pretty Chinese women, their mission to marry Tibetan men in hope of diluting pure Tibetan blood with their offspring.

These reasons and many others was why I choose to take covert photos for the Tibetan government, and why I choose to deliver the stack of hidden letters I had carried from India to Nepal and now to Lhasa, not forgetting a certain shade of lipstick.

Finding the Chinese hotels being built upon pledged land photos were taken. I made for Barkhor Square and police check points there.

With shots of a Buddhist monk having his bag searched by the Chinese army, and with other Tibetans being searched so they may enter the land their oppressors had agreed to be theirs, I took a final photo of a police commissioner standing in front of me, his eyes on my camera resting on my hip as I pointed my lens at him and took a single frame.

So came a handing over of letters from one cousin to another. With phone calls and emails forbidden under threat of a heavy prison sentence, it was important to deliver these letters of family news.

A phone number given to me in India was rung and within an hour the letter's recipient arrived in my hotel lobby. Much delight came in receiving those letters smuggled into a country of such oppression - with a lipstick bringing as much joy.

Relieved my quest was complete and I no longer carried such illegal contraband, the one I had delivered everything to reached into her bag. She smiled on handing me a similar sized stack of letters to be returned to the cousin in India.

Agreeing to do so I considered my choices a few days later when standing for another very long twenty minutes at Lhasa airport's immigration counter; a fresh stack of contraband letters in my backpack and a small memory stick full of clandestine photos stitched into its side.

Allowed to board my plane to Kathmandu, three weeks later I was back in India, where the Tibetan Parliament in Exile received their photos, and once again I saw the smiles of another on receiving letters from a cousin of long missed homelands.

Chapter Eight

Indonesia

A Taste of Sulphur

Ijen Volcano
Java
Indonesia
1am - 2015

I stumbled in the dark again.

This 1am climb on a narrow, muddy path weaving its way up the side of an active volcano really was a once in a lifetime experience. I would not be doing this by choice ever again.

The others of our group were ahead. No longer able to see the beams of their torches I scolded myself for not bringing my own. I questioned why I was ascending one of Indonesia's more active volcanos.

Indonesia had become another second home for me. The capital of Jakarta now stood beside Bangkok, Kathmandu and Delhi; places ideal for regrouping and stumbling into where the next adventure was going to be. There was another reason for being here. Visas sometimes became a problem.

Some countries only allowed short periods of stay.

Nepal only allows its western visitors three months in one calendar year, and Thailand's visa allowances are now much stricter than when living there for three years in the early 2000s.

For those three years living in Thailand each month would involve hiring a jeep and driving northwards from Thailand's northern city of Chiang Mai to the town of Mai Sai on the Burmese border.

Leaving Thailand and entering Myanmar, Burmese immigration would ask if you wanted to go shopping. This meant visiting Myanmar's markets before being stamped back into Thailand for another month – until having to repeat the process again thirty days later.

I never minded these visa runs. Myanmar's markets were filled with the latest music and movies all available then on pirated CD or DVD. The drive home always provided a sunset resting above northern Thailand's jungle forest canopies, an ideal accompaniment for new music bought.

Bouncing between these countries suited me. Soon I had a barber and coffee shop in all mentioned second homes. Each aware of what I required.

Now it was Jakarta's turn to become host. Wanderlust soon appeared and a journey was made eastwards across the island of Java - from Jakarta to Yogyakarta to Malang and now Ijen near Java's eastern coastline. This was how I wound up climbing this god forsaken volcano in darkness.

Ijen volcano's pull on tourists was to see the sulphur miners at work chipping away at gigantic yellow blocks of sulphur, the byproduct of this volcano's might.

By 4am I looked down from the lip of Ijen volcano. Dawn light broke over a bright turquoise lake at Ijen's base, its water's vivid colour the result of its high sulfuric acid concentration.

It was what was on the banks of the world's largest acidic crater lake I had come to see. This meant making a 2,624 feet/800 metre decent by narrow stone pathway before reaching Ijen's bright yellow sulphur supplies at its base, and the miners I had come to photograph who toiled there.

Beginning the decent I was more worried about being able to capture the scene in such poor light than the sheer drop at my side.

Down into the depths of sulphur clouds, flashes of 16 feet/5 metre high blue flames accompanied me, a result of gas condensing into liquid and igniting.

With a gas mask rented for $5 the effects of surrounding sulfuric mists eased, although uncovered eyes still succumbed to a swirling fume's bite and vicious sting.

With the crater's base at last reached the light needed for my camera arrived also. Poisonous vapours settled for a moment to reveal the miners I had come to document.

While some hacked away at huge blocks of yellow sulphur solidifying beside an acidic lake, others loaded two baskets on either end of a wooden pole with their hoard.

Filling two baskets with as many sulphur blocks as possible, those baskets were then hoisted up with the wooden pole cast across strong shoulders, their yellow prize set in balance on either side. Then a march back up the hazardous track I had taken would ensue.

Where my gas mask provided me with adequate breathing these miners had no such protection. Only a wet rag wrapped across nose and mouth provided any relief from noxious fumes worked within, their eyes suffering the same sting as all present.

This would be the first of two trips these miners would make each day. A climb out of the crater and another half mile walk to Ijen's weighing station. Carrying up to ninety kilos across their back, for each grueling trip a miner is paid an average of $7 for every sulphur load delivered.

Once processed the sulphur is used to bleach sugar, make matches, fertiliser and to vulcanise rubber. There seems no other way for this commodity to be transported from the Ijen volcano's bowels except on the shoulders of Ijen's sulphur miners. Shoulders of which tell a story of each miner; a pronounced mass of muscle appearing out of place on that of an Indonesian's natural, slight build.

With photographs taken from the crater's ridge of an acid lake and plumes of yellow smoke surrounding Ijen's miners, there would be two poignant portraits taken of those working in these extreme conditions. Each frame gave a different perspective on those who mined Ijen's natural resources. The first was of a younger man taking a well-earned break halfway up the crater's steep incline.

Smoking a cigarette with hand on hip, an air of relief hung about him as his work place in the background continued to bellow poisonous vapours, a fog reminiscent of yellow tinged electrical storm clouds that sometimes gather in a South East Asian monsoon.

The second portrait was on climbing up out of Ijen's crater.

An older man stumbled ahead. Each footstep an obvious battle, he shuffled forwards intent on receiving the paltry wage for his troubles.

Years of carrying out such a task in order to feed his family had taken its toll. This was seen in the eyes of one who had once taken to his task with ease as a younger man. Now it appeared the extreme weight balanced across him proved an unimaginable bane.

One of the last remaining active sulphur mines in the world, Ijen has become a controversial tourist attraction. Over four thousand visitors a year pay tour companies to walk on Ijen's crater floor. Little goes to those who are watched and photographed in their hardship, but for the occasional tip from a tourist's hand for posed photographs.

The future of Ijen volcano as both a mining site and tourist attraction is unclear.

Seventy-five percent of the world's active volcanoes are located in Indonesia. Up to ninety percent of all worldwide earthquakes occur in the region. With Indonesia's positioning on the 25,000 mile/ 40,200km belt of the Ring of Fire, it remains to be seen if Kawah Ijen volcano is ready to erupt once again after its last display of force in 1999.

It would be another seismic fault which would send me in a new direction, far away from the heat and humidity of South East Asia; two tectonic plates in constant flux playing their part beneath the Himalaya mountain range I had become accustomed to seeing over the years.

The afternoon of my return to Ijen's coffee plantation I learnt of the 7.8 magnitude earthquake which had struck Nepal. I instinctively knew I had to get myself back to Kathmandu.

Leaving the island of Java behind and arriving on Bali by boat, after a few nights on the north of the island my want to return to Nepal grew. I bought a flight to Bangkok.

Spending a single monsoon night in Bangkok saw me boarding the first available plane to the Nepalese capital the following day - a quarter full flight composing of doctors, Thai disaster relief teams, a handful of orange robed Buddhist monks, and me with my camera bag sitting on my lap.

Chapter Nine

Nepal

A Lunchtime Earthquake

Thamel
Kathmandu
Nepal
2015

Walking out from Kathmandu airport I met with a hundred stares.

In front of the airport's exit bemused taxi drivers gazed, confused at how the day had brought them a customer. Fifty metres to my right at Kathmandu's airport entrance a queue of hundreds craned their necks. All looking at the lone traveller arriving into the country they now tried so hard to leave.

Hoisting a backpack over one shoulder and a camera bag over the other I found a taxi to take me to Kathmandu's tourist area of Thamel. I was unsure as to what I would find.

Flying in from Bangkok, Kathmandu's immigration was quick and easy. I was one of only a few travellers requesting a tourist visa that day. The baggage carousel proved of ease also - my backpack was easily found amid boxes of medical equipment with a large red cross on a white background on its side.

It was five days after Nepal had met with a with a magnitude 7.8 to 8.1 earthquake which had claimed almost 9,000 lives, left 22,000 injured and caused over three million to become homeless.

The earthquake's epicentre had been in the Gorkha region of Nepal, some 50 miles/80km north west of the capital.

Kathmandu showed its results.

In a street of small redbrick homes most remained intact, yet there would be one house completely destroyed with no rhyme or reason as to why. The damage in Kathmandu was sporadic. However, where that damage was it was catastrophic.

Finding a hotel to stay the night I then took a walk down much remembered streets towards Durbar Square.

Durbar Square had always been a place I would walk around. This collection of temples, shrines and tall wooden buildings of two or three tiers displayed the skills of Newari artists and craftsmen over several centuries. Each structure sat on steep stone steps in front of what had once been Nepal's Royal Palace. These wooden constructions were no more. Reduced to an aged heap of what had once been ornately carved wooden beam and masonry.

I had often climbed those old temple steps which had surrendered to the April 25th earthquake. The photographs taken from those heights months earlier had been deleted to make more memory space on my laptop, thinking I could take them again on my next visit.

I would stay in four different hotels in four nights until finding one which suited me. At last finding a hotel without a long crack running from floor to ceiling and back down the opposite wall.

My fifth hotel room was on the fifth floor in the centre of Thamel. With two single beds, a small TV and a settee and desk I decided to stay.

Spending the next couple of weeks walking around the Nepalese capital I documented a damaged city.

With days spent taking photographs, processing them on my laptop and sending them to agencies, I also watched Thamel's tourists slowly ebb away from once vibrant, busy streets and lanes.

At 12:50pm on the 12th May 2015 Nepal was struck by a second earthquake. I had been in Kathmandu less than two weeks.

Taking a break on my bed watching the movie Tomb Raider on TV, I looked across my room to the laptop worked on all morning. Its screen began to shake. As did everything else around me.

There had been several tremors since my arrival in Kathmandu. Most would be on their way after a few seconds. This felt different.

Waiting for an end to the roar of tectonic plates grinding together, I wondered why I had chosen a fifth floor hotel room in a city where a 7.8 magnitude earthquake had struck less than a month earlier.

Those roars evolved into a rolling thunder, a sound growing in the same intensity as my room's judders and jolts.

This would be my fourth earthquake having experienced three in the space of six months over a decade ago. The first being in Nepal when visiting the lakeside town of Pokhara in 2004. I had been in bed at the time, as had I when encountering Central American tremors in Costa Rica a few months later. This seemed to be a common factor as I was shaken awake one Boxing Day morning whilst living in Chiang Mai, the result of Thailand's 2004 tsunami.

This time I was on the bed not in it. I was soon off it.

Deciding it may be a good idea to leave, the room's shudder subdued as I stood, only to be replaced by the earthquake phenomenon of liquefaction.

The earthquake had caused so much stress in the ground under Kathmandu that its soil particles had begun to move in respect to each other, so giving a similar effect as that of water.

This liquefaction resulted in transforming my hotel into a boat on stormy waters, the floor undulating in waves beneath me as I reached for my camera bag and made for the door and to the relative safety of the streets below.

As the earthquake's roar continued I left my fifth floor room with my camera bag slung across my shoulder. For some reason I tried to lock the padlock on my room's door. My hands were shaking and I just couldn't get the key into its home. My trial was brought to a halt by the hotel housekeeper who ushered me down an ever moving staircase leading to supposed safety.

Stepping from the hotel entrance the roars and tremors which had accompanied my escape began to subside. This could not be said for the panic encountered on the streets of Thamel.

Motorbikes, bicycles and taxi cabs weaved between masses of people either staring up at the buildings around them or running in every direction possible.

There are said to be four things people do when in a disaster situation. They either run away, run around in circles, stand still or race to help others. I am sure in saying we all like to think we would forsake our own safety to aid another's distress, but you only find out which of the four actions you will take by being in a disaster setting.

I have found my reaction. It is one I can never escape from. On every occasion when in danger I have stood still. Frozen to the spot. Even though my reaction only lasts for only a few seconds I'm thankful I don't run round in circles.

My camera was now in my hands and I began to shoot. As always any fear left me. My camera once again guided me to stillness. The shaking hands which had hindered my attempt of lock and key only moments earlier disappeared completely. I was left with a great sense of calm as the world plunged into chaos around me. Now I was just an observer. Detached from all surrounding.

Sidestepping those trying to find open ground away from already structurally damaged buildings I made for the places others escaped, calmness still about me coupled with a hunter's instinct to capture the intrinsic heart of these moments. To document and portray what lay before me. To get that one photo.

With camera settled in my hand I returned to the stillness encountered in a conflict zone of Myanmar and standing before those Chinese police checkpoints of Tibet. Now I was focused and at peace as the world descended into chaos.

Kathmandu raised two metres in altitude that Wednesday lunch time, all at the cost of Mount Everest losing two metres off its summit. I suppose those two metres had to go somewhere.

For those tourists still staying in Nepal it seemed a 7.3 magnitude jolt was enough to prompt their want to leave. Earthquake or aftershock it didn't matter and they began their exodus to safer land.

India had opened its Sunauli borders allowing visitors to Nepal to enter India visa free. This was a couple of years before a visa on arrival option had been introduced and many took advantage of this situation.

The streets of Thamel were busy again, though only with tourists making a hasty escape. An erratic chase through streets filled with traffic heading for open spaces away from Thamel's tall buildings. I was going nowhere. My intuition told me I was where I was supposed to be. As ever I followed my instincts.

Tourists were not the only ones to leave the city. Kathmandu's population of monkeys also alighted after April's earthquake.

Escaping into the jungle forests surrounding Kathmandu Valley they would not be seen until a few months later. It would take a good year until they all returned to the capital's temples, streets and parks.

After a couple of hours wandering Thamel's surrounding area capturing Nepal's second earthquake with my camera, I was left with numerous photographs showing the results of Nepal's second shake. Now I had to somehow get them sent out into the world.

There were two problems to face. My laptop was still in my fifth floor hotel room, and with a power cut throughout the city it would be difficult to find any functioning Wi-Fi.

Running up my hotel's five flights in darkness to retrieve my laptop I was greeted by the hotel manager on my way out..

"Here," the hotel manager said, his hand outstretched towards me. "You are in charge," he placed a set of keys in my hand.

"In charge of what?"

"The hotel, I am going to my family in my village."

With that he was gone.

Still a little shaken by the events unfolding I just put those keys in my pocket and started my hunt for Wi-Fi. Somehow I found some.

A back street hotel had internet. I don't know how but it did. Sitting on the hotel's front steps I began to send my photos to London, aware of the time limit on these vital shots.

One of Kathmandu's many street dogs approached me. Nestling down beside me, his head rested on my foot. A comfort I am sure for us both. The hotel owner took a photo of the scene. To this day I don't know who looks more anxious, me or the dog.

Walking back to my hotel I was now in charge of I passed by another hotel; one I recalled from my first days in Nepal eleven years earlier. A few people sat in its courtyard of green wooden tables and chairs. I joined them.

An American resident there saw the consoling I needed as much as the street dog had. He gave me a bottle of coke. Even though it was just a drink it was a kindness I have never forgotten.

Rested, I went back to my hotel. I was welcomed by its two other guests. Each had heard it was me who was now in charge and asked for my phone number in case they needed anything. Too tired to protest I gave it them before returning to my room and falling asleep.

*

A familiar rumble and shake woke me in the early hours. With another aftershock an hour later reaching a magnitude of 6 there was a knock at my door. It was one of the other residents telling me we should all sleep downstairs.

Begrudgingly I agreed. At the reception we were joined by *my* hotel's other equally unwilling guest, a Japanese tourist who kept insisting these aftershocks were nothing with calls of "I am from Japan" every ten minutes.

With a chorus of snores I couldn't sleep in the reception and found a store cupboard with enough room for me to curl up in.

Waking the next morning I looked up to the shelves I had slept beneath. Each was filled with heavy pots of paint. I was glad there hadn't been another earthquake in the night and I hadn't woken up more colourful than I was before going to sleep.

Thamel's streets were quieter than ever that morning. The only pedestrians were those with suitcases and backpacks making a dash for the airport flanked by closed shops.

Not wanting to spend another night in a cupboard I set about finding a new home. I went to the hotel where I had been given a coke the day before. Within the hour I was moved in.

That hotel room would become a home for the next three years. A base which I would return to each time after venturing into India or South East Asia.

I left the keys of *my* hotel for the night with its housekeeper, the one met on the stairs in our escape from the earthquake the previous day.

From then on we would see each other occasionally on Thamel's streets. We would give one another a nod and a smile before continuing onwards, each of us aware of the unique bond held in a shared moment of fear.

That evening I sat eating dinner when my phone rang.

"Hello, where are you?" A man said.

I recognised his voice. It was one of the guests from the hotel I had run for one night.

"I'm having dinner," I replied.

"Well when you have finished," he said, "I need new towels."

Chapter Ten

AMERICA

Kennedy, Trains and New Freedoms

America – (32 States)
1976 - 2002

America has always been part of my travel itinerary. Thirty-two states visited already. A remaining eighteen to be seen at a future date.

A first arrival to the US came in 1976 with parents. Staying with family friends in Pennsylvania, their neighbour offered an opportunity to meet his niece in Washington DC. The niece was the personal secretary to Senator Edward Kennedy in his office in the Capitol Building - the meeting place of the United States Congress and seat of the U.S. federal government.

An eventual arrival to Washington DC saw myself and my parents enter the office building to the left of the Capitol Building. There we met with Edward Kennedy's secretary in said senator's office.

Kennedy himself was not present. The primaries for an approaching presidential election were on, a presidency which eventually went to Jimmy Carter. My dad noticed a framed photo beside the senator's desk. It was of Ted Kennedy's older brother John. It was who stood beside the late president that caught my parents' attention.

Standing side by side and caught in a moment of laughter, John F. Kennedy stood with Lord Harlech, once elected Member of Parliament for our small home town.

Telling our host of the coincidence we were invited to delve further into the home of American politics. This involved taking an elevator to the basement where a small train was boarded and we were carried under Washington DC's highways and into the US Senate. Once through the briefest of security we sat in the Senate's public gallery to watch the US government at play.

With another journey to the US in 1979 I would not visit America for another thirteen years.

Flying into New York at the age of twenty-two, a six week train pass was bought allowing for travel by day or night for almost half of the country; the northeast, mid-east and the south.

With a visit southwards to the American capital a return to New York saw to boarding a night train to Chicago - travelling at night opposed to day allowed for not dipping into what little funds were already carried. Tucked into a reclining seat, a coat for a pillow and a backpack for a foot rest was often as comfortable as a youth hostel's twenty bed dorm.

Travelling South from Chicago stops were made in Memphis to see Elvis' extravagant home, and from there to New Orleans with a few nights spent on an infamous Bourbon Street - $10 for a cigar, handed over by a showgirl after rolling it on her thigh in front of you.

Heading back north through Georgia and South and North Carolina, I returned to Washington DC and the youth hostel first stayed in a month earlier. I was offered a free bed for the night if I answered the phone and made breakfast for the guests. I lasted three days having burnt everyone's breakfast three days running.

It was back on the train. This time Boston was my destination.

Another night train booked from Washington DC to Boston meant a midnight arrival to New York's Grand Central Station on Halloween. I remember waking to see all of horror's perpetrators sitting around my carriage in elaborate Halloween costume.

I fell asleep as the train continued north. Waking six hours later I captured a freedom once found in Paris six years earlier.

Wrapped in a blue wool jumper knitted by the one I had rung from halfway up the Eiffel Tower and with my legs balanced on my backpack, I stared at the view I had woken to.

A small harbour played host to several small boats. Those boats were lit by an emerging dawn light of light turquoise and soft blues. A sense of oneness surrounded me. There was just me and my backpack. I was free from all constraints. That morning liberty unveiled her much favoured nomadic life to me.

In that moment wanderlust became a constant companion. At times a joy, yet also a burden, wanderlust's touch would now always be on me. It took many years to accept this want to wander and roam the world. That such cravings for travel would always be with me. It was only in that acceptance that I became truly free.

A stay in Boston evolved into myself and friends hiring a minibus and travelling to Cape Cod with an eventual stay on Martha's Vineyard – all in the depths of autumn.

With a return to New York and an almost missed flight home to England, I arrived back and started a new career as a hairdresser.

Between 1992 and 1996 I trained in one of London's top salons, learnt what I had to and returned home, where a year later I discovered I liked cutting men's hair instead of all those perms and colours and opened my own barber shop.

After working hard building up a clientele over six months the wanderlust began to itch. That itch soon developed into a scratch. A sign was put up in my shop window explaining I would be back in one month's time. The next day I landed in Miami, Florida. Another train pass was bought. This time for the whole of America.

On my first day I was cutting hair on Miami Beach. Even now I always carry my scissors with me in my backpack. Rooftops in China and balconies in both Cambodia and India have been locations for my scissors and comb, one memorable setting was on a beach in Fiji overlooking crystal clear waters, my client sitting on an upturned bin.

From Miami I travelled north to the top of Florida then headed west towards California. Travelling through Alabama, Mississippi and Louisiana, I stayed awhile in New Orleans where another showgirl handed me a cigar. Texas was my next stop.

After visiting the canals and streets of San Antonia, El Paso in Texas' far western corner became a new destination. From there I travelled into Mexico. After a week in the country travelling around a quarter of the way down I made back to America, in haste. My entry point was to be Arizona, but first I had to get through the notorious border crossing of Nogales – a tale deserving of its own chapter.

I at last arrived in California.

Los Angeles was a city new to me.

From the first moment I adored the place. LA would become a slight second home for me, long before I ever walked on Bangkok's steamy streets.

My trainers fell apart outside the Chinese Mann's Theatre in central Hollywood – just as I was placing a foot in Harrison Ford's concrete shoe print. There was no time to buy another pair, my train to Seattle was leaving in less than an hour.

I boarded the train just in time, battling to keep my backpack steady whilst rushing in flip flops. Being a smoker at the time I would wait until the train at last stopped for smokers to step down from their ride and get their fix. This was great while still in sunny California, but as the train travelled further north smokers were greeted with four foot of snow. I still partook in flip flops, my bare feet ice cold.

With five days exploring Seattle, one month after my arrival in New York I flew home after travelling by train from Miami, through America's southern states, with a dip into Mexico before heading north along the America's Pacific coast.

Returning home and to my barber shop, I regained my clientele, began to employ staff, bought a house, a car, and all the trappings. I lasted just under six years until wanderlust called on me again. To be honest that want for travel had begun its call the second year into having the shop. I ignored it to my peril. Be warned, wanderlust will be surrendered to sooner or later, as it demands.

So in the fifth year of my shop I took a nine month break where I flew to Australia, flipped coins of where to go next from Hawaii to Fiji to The Cook Islands and finally to Los Angeles, where it seemed as if I had come full circle standing in Harrison's Hollywood footstep once more – this time in new trainers.

Chapter Eleven

Myanmar

Kalashnikovs and a Duty of Care

**KNLA Training Camp,
Undisclosed Location,
Myanmar
May 2005**

After a five hour drive by rented jeep I arrived at the Thai/Burmese border town of Mae Sot.

Along with a journalist and another photographer we had made our way from northern Thailand to the small border town.

Photographing Mae Sot's annual three day boxing event a week earlier we had met a member of the Karen National Liberation Army (KNLA) - a military faction opposed to the Myanmar government.

This is why we had returned to Mae Sot. This was our story. A unique invitation to visit the KNLA's training camp. An invite which would take us across the Irrawaddy River's flowing waters at dawn to an undisclosed location deep within Myanmar's jungle forest.

Our contact was a captain in the KNLA. He had invited us to document his soldiers in want of promoting his cause.

The military branch of the Karen National Union, the KNLA has been fighting against their government and defending Karen State communities and culture within eastern Myanmar for over sixty years.

When Myanmar gained independence from the British in 1948 tensions ran high between the Myanmar government and the Karen community. With the Karen wanting independence from Myanmar the Karen National Defence Organisation (KNDO) was formed.

Later becoming the KNLA, the KNDO was an armed organisation formed to protect the welfare and traditions of the Karen people, the majority of its soldiers having served alongside the British Army in Myanmar during World War II.

Dominating townships around Rangoon (now Yangon) in the early 1950's the eventual arrest of Karen political leaders and a lack of guns and supplies caused the KNLA to retreat to the southwest of the country. There they continued their fight, attaining the stigma of being the world's longest running civil war.

The day after our arrival as dusk gave way to early morning light we were driven from Mae Sot and along narrow dust track roads until reaching Thailand's banks of the Irrawaddy River. It was here we met with our guide, a cousin to the captain met a week earlier.

Myanmar lay one hundred feet away across turbulent waters. I looked to the bamboo raft which would take us across the Irrawaddy. Any apprehension to what we were going into was lost. My concerns were towards not getting my camera bag wet.

There were no incidents on our crossing. In fact it was quite enjoyable as the river fell into a smooth flow. My mind wandered and I forgot we were about to enter a conflict zone.

My thoughts were soon brought abruptly back. Two men stepped from the undergrowth as our raft moored onto Myanmar soil.

They had appeared from no-where. I hadn't seen any hint of them before, but I suppose they were dressed in camouflage.

Stepping from the raft and onto a new country I reached for my camera and took a photo of them both.

One was an expressionless man in his late forties hugging a rocket propelled grenade launcher (RPG) close to him, the other was barely a teenager, a prized Kalashnikov held proudly against his chest.

It was they who guided us into the KNLA's training camp through dense jungle until meeting with a wide expanse of parched grassland, its perimeter dotted with wooden shack homes for soldiers and their families.

Greeted with puzzled stares, residents of the training camp had not been told of their new visitors. Bemusement was soon replaced by curiosity and we were welcomed into the heart of the community.

Of the hundred or so who called their camp a home most were families, all of which went about their usual business of laundry and food preparations, shaded from the day's building sunlight beneath small awnings spanning out from teak wood slatted porches.

The man with the RPG was constantly at our side. As was the boy not yet old enough to shave. The families paid no attention to the armoury around them. Carrying on with life as if this was the norm, which I suppose to them it was.

We were given a plate of rice and curried meat before being ushered to the other side of the camp to eat. Dutifully carrying the meal I had no intention of eating we were joined by another westerner no older than my own thirty-five years.

Sitting down together he devoured his lunch. He was obviously used to the food. He told us he had been living in the camp for the last three months, teaching the KNLA all he had learnt in his recent time in the French Foreign Legion.

I found it quite exciting. I had met a Legionnaire. A mercenary, a gun for hire. There was however something not quite right about him. Speaking in a monotone French drawl his eyes held the same blackness as his polished boots and black combat attire.

"No pictures of me," he pointed at my camera.

I nodded. I didn't want to talk to him. I didn't really want to talk to anyone.

This was when I discovered the power of familiarity. I decided not to form any kind of emotional bridge with him or any of these people I had come to photograph. I was aware that if I did communicate with anyone here, if something went wrong or if things got heated it would be easier for them to cross that bridge. So I kept an aloof distance. An action I was thankful of in the unforeseen events to come at the end of the day.

We were shown around the camp, leaving the Legionnaire behind to finish the meal I had not touched.

As he focused on his second helping I tilted my camera at my hip and got a photograph of him without his knowledge, my own feistiness coming through on being told what I could and could not take photographs of. A trait which would land me in many troublesome situations in unforeseen future years to come.

Walking through the camp more soldiers joined us. I took photos of guns wielded in action and young soldiers holding worn Russian rifles, each boy filled with pride they were to be seen by the rest of the world.

Directed further around the camp it became apparent the bulk of this liberation army was made up of children aged between twelve and fifteen years old. Each was the owner of a uniform and rifle. Even those yet able to talk carried plastic toy guns, emulating brothers and fathers as they played around their mother's ankles.

This was the setting I found myself in now. A place where children were given guns, trained to kill and instilled with loathing towards their government. Although not all these child soldiers came from the safe family units I had witnessed on my arrival.

Most of these gun touting pre-adults were themselves victims of the civil war they now found themselves embroiled within. Parentless children who had been taken under the wing of those whose mission was to fight those in power by any means possible with an assortment of weaponry at hand.

Looking out onto the camp's far edges I was aware of the landmines placed there by the KNLA to keep Myanmar's official army from entering the camp. The official army watching now from the steep jungle hillsides surrounding us.

My emotional bridge became longer. I avoided eye contact with our hosts, except with my camera. I still took as many photos as I could without care of how close I got to my subjects. With my camera raised I was shielded and calm reigned within me.

As our tour came to a close we posed for a group photo. I can be seen smiling away crouched down at the front, guns and RPG behind me. In that moment all seemed like a movie set walked onto. There I was in t-shirt, shorts and flip-flops. Being offered a flak vest and helmet on arrival I had declined. It was too hot to wear those cumbersome items - vest too heavy, helmet too big.

After a tour of the camp we were led to a large two story house on the outer edge of the camp. Told no photos were allowed inside the house I lowered my camera, but kept it switched on.

Taken upstairs and led into a room we sat facing a hospital bed where a pretty young nurse saw to the elderly man lying beneath its sheets. The old man was General Bo Mya.

From 1944 to 1945 General Bo Mya had fought with the British Army against the Japanese in the Dawna Hills, a mountain range in eastern Myanmar. After the Karen declared independence from Burma in 1949 he rose to power within the Karen movement until controlling the Karen National Union's military wing - the KNLA.

Now he was a man in the closing moments of his life, yet still he commanded a power of authority sensed within the room. The stillness felt for most of the day escaped me.

I saw through it all. I saw how the KNLA were not the underdogs or the good guys fighting oppression. They were just as ruthless as any liberation army found across the world. This was evident in their carefree use of children to fight their battles.

Making my apologies I stood and left the room.

Venturing outside I sat in the shade and looked out across hillsides I knew were filled with government soldiers, all as eager to pull the trigger on their guns as the child soldiers within the camp grounds where I now sat.

My thoughts returned to those encountered throughout the day. I at last identified what had been troubling me with each photo taken.

It is said the eyes are a window of the soul. On this occasion it was. The stares of each child soldier met with held the same darkness and lack of emotion seen within the eyes of a Legionnaire met.

This was the legacy of their KNLA training. A stripping away of emotion and a snatching away of the joys of the young. An embitterment of easily influenced and yet to be developed minds. All in aid of becoming pawns in an old man's war.

I was joined by the one who had guided our passage across the river and into their gun strewn environment.

I looked to them and smiled. I toughened up in those moments. It was me after all who had chosen to come here. I could have said no at any moment, played it safe and stayed at home. Taking responsibility for my own actions and choices made the peace of mind I searched for arrive. It faltered as my guide spoke to me.

"What's the matter?"

"Nothing," I shrugged.

"No. What is wrong?" They pressed.

That was it. I knew they knew I saw through their façade. That I had seen past the romance of a liberation army fighting against government domination. That I had identified the pollution of young minds in order for them to fight for their cause. I had to think fast.

"I've got girlfriend problems," I said.

I wanted to smile at their confused stare.

"You have girlfriend problems?"

"Yes," I said. In fact I had at the time. Then at all came out.

As I spoke it changed from me trying to get out of a lethal situation to pouring my heart out to this stranger about the heartache I was experiencing, so much so I forgot all about the guns, the landmines and the revered General I had left upstairs and shown great disrespect to in leaving. I just talked on and on and on.

"Ok, ok," I was interrupted in my tales of unrequited love.

It was obvious my guide had had enough of listening to my woes.

"I'm sure you'll be fine," they told me with a pat on my shoulder before walking back into the house and leaving me alone once more.

It had worked. I couldn't believe it.

Our drive back to northern Thailand was filled with tales of the day and of the intricacies of the KNLA's strategies and purpose.

I held no interest in the politics of the situation. I had my photos. I had successfully captured the day. Although this mattered little as my conscience played heavy on me.

I understood that if those child soldiers were identified through my photos then they would be routinely executed; an act of nipping the bud before the bloom.

"I'm not publishing the photos," I said from the backseat.

I took rest in the brief silence filling the jeep. I knew what was to come. Finding a strength never met with before I stuck to my decision through all the words said in order to change my mind.

"Duty of care," the other photographer said.

I had never heard of the expression before, but it instilled the responsibility I held within the photographs taken that day, and of future photographs yet to be taken.

"It's up to you," the journalist eventually said.

Although my decision not to publish those photos saw an end to my brief venture into the world of documentary photography, I had cut my teeth and knew I wanted more.

Chapter Twelve

The Cook Islands

Scooters, Scars and Sea Slugs

Rarotonga
The Cook Islands
2002

A flip of a coin saw me land in The Cook Islands.

The idyllic Fijian beach on which that coin was flipped lay fourteen hundred miles southwest and a three hour flight away.

Invited to join five others to travel to The Cook Islands, all watched my coin throw to aid my decision; I was thankful I had chosen heads and not tails - if the coin had landed tails it would have meant an immediate flight home. I had more to discover yet.

Found in the near centre of the South Pacific, The Cook Islands are a collection of fifteen islands scattered over a vast area. The largest of these islands is Rarotonga with a population of just under eighteen thousand. This is where I and five others found ourselves

A guest house with a short walk from the beach was found at the south of the island. Scooters were hired - with a warning.

A common accident for visitors to meet with when hiring a scooter was when a hot exhaust pipe met with a rider's shins.

This left a distinct scar in the shape of the island. Hence the name given to such a burn – a Rarotonga Tattoo.

Despite being near Rarotonga's coastline the guest house was in a jungle setting. Within the garden a pagoda protected those beneath occasional harsh tropical rains, and the guest house held a long corridor of which rooms were placed on either side. On our second day a scream came from that corridor. All guests rushed to see a pale backpacker pointing to what she had discovered. An eight inch Huntsman spider made its way between the guest house's rooms to the other end of the corridor.

"There he is," our home's manager smiled behind us. "We've been looking for him all week." - but the spider was gone by the time he went to catch it, leaving an element of fear when reaching into your backpack or putting on trainers each morning.

Exploring the island proved easy. Just one main road circumnavigated Rarotonga. A complete circle which took around forty-five minutes to complete. The only obstacles were stray dogs meandering across the road, or the fright of riding close to an airport runway's end when an airplane passed over close enough to touch.

Even though the beach at the south of the island was beautiful it was a little peculiar.

From fine beach sands knee high warm seawater stretched out towards the Pacific Ocean for one hundred metres. A low flat stone wall two metres wide and one metre high was the only defense between that knee high water and a two mile plus drop straight down to the ocean floor.

A group of us stood at that ocean wall. Waves three times our height rose up, curled then broke just before our barrier from the depths. Trying to grasp why the waves never struck us my thoughts were elsewhere. I had another concern.

My hundred metre journey from beachfront to tall waves had been one of concentration. Long black sea slugs lay every three feet in all directions. Rarotonga's white sandy floor was covered in them. I only trod on one once - its squidgy black body squeezing effortlessly up between my toes.

Days were spent on the beach and evenings riding scooters to various bars around the island. On those bars sat glass bowls filled with small white flowers - a bud to be placed behind the ear. Left ear denoting being in a relationship, right for being up for grabs.

In one bar a map of the world hung by small brass nails in each of its four corners. Only then did I truly see where I was; so far from land and in the middle of the Pacific's immense waters.

Three days into my stay a choice was made to ride scooters to the centre of the island. Meeting with a path filled with thick mud my scooter became stuck. I climbed off and watched it fall on its side. Leaning forward I stumbled and fell forward.

The searing pain across my shins meant only one thing. I had got myself not one but two Rarotonga Tattoos.

I stared down at two pink island shaped wounds. They were all the more prominent on Fiji tanned legs. Looking to the offending scooter exhaust pipe it also shared those two island shapes, this time in the form of my sizzling skin.

Visiting a hospital and receiving surprised looks from a nurse there having never seen someone burn both shins at once, my legs were bandaged and a scooter was returned.

For two days I applied given ointment and changed stained bandages. There was no improvement.

I rented another scooter. Passing by my old one on the way to the rental office I saw its shiny exhaust was now tainted by two Rarotonga shaped blemishes.

With legs still unhealed I packed my backpack and boarded a small plane to the island of Aitutaki. With only room for eight people the plane's coveted front seat was taken by the pilot's dog.

Only an hour flight north of Rarotonga, Aitutaki is home to only a couple of thousand people. This small island is surrounded by a coral barrier reef teeming with marine life of rays, angelfish and turtles.

I would walk on white sand beaches where coconut trees lined my path. Those trees hosted a metal sheet wrapped halfway around its trunk. This was to defend its bounty from the island's coconut crabs whose one gigantic claw was powerful enough to open a desired coconut with one pinch.

Evenings were spent sitting on moonlit beaches talking with other travellers met, looking out ono the Pacific's far horizon, the upside down star constellation of The Plough hovering just above the ocean.

My legs had still not healed as I boarded a boat for the day bound for One Foot Island. A place where all visitors are told to bring their passport.

So called as from above the island resembles a large left foot, One

Foot Island is about two hundred metres long and one hundred metres wide at its widest point.

The boat ride took less than an hour. As all passengers stepped onto this stunning desert island our passports were stamped with One Foot Island's official hallmark. Unbeknown to me then, that stamp would allow me entry into Canada a month from now.

Crossing from America into Canada, immigration studied my passport now filled with eight months of travels. Pulled aside I was asked why I was travelling and where I was going in Canada. Sure I wasn't going to be allowed into the country the immigration lady leafing through my passport stopped.

"One Foot Island, I've been there too," she said handing me my passport and ushering me into her country.

But for now I was on One Foot Island.

Boarding our boat I watched the others dive into a crystal clear lagoon. One of the crew asked me why I didn't join them. I showed him my unhealed shins.

"Take your bandages off and put your legs in the water," he said. "You will see," he added on seeing my hesitation.

It took only a minute for them to appear. Each fish was a vision of vivid colour and shape. I watched a rainbow of fins fight for place as each fish ate away at my wounds' dead skin.

After a five or so minutes their meal was over and my shins looked better than they had for days - the tropical humidity of the South Pacific can hinder the healing process.

Returning to Rarotonga another coin flip came. It was heads again. Home could wait a little while longer.

I boarded a plane for Los Angeles. Following my arrival those Rarotonga tattoos healed within days.

To this day faint tender outlines remain across my shins. Each faded scar a physical reminder of treasured memories.

Chapter Thirteen

Mexico

A Copper Canyon Journey

Ciudad Juárez
Mexico
1996

I have travelled in Mexico twice.

The second time was in 2004. A two day stay in Tulum, Southern Mexico, before journeying through Central America - Mexico to Belize to Guatemala to Honduras, Nicaragua and finally Costa Rica. A six month trip prompting a return to the Asian climes I knew best.

My first trip in 1996 was more comprehensive.

On a one month long trip across America from Miami to Seattle by train I left the comfort of Texan city San Antonio and arrived in El Paso. From there I ventured southwards into Mexico. Leaving El Paso I entered the Mexican border town of Ciudad Juárez.

I was eventually allowed into Mexico by a policeman complete with unbuttoned shirt and mirrored sunglasses hovering above a drooping mustache - stereotypes are stereotypes for a reason.

Stepping into searing heat I caught a bus heading south to the city of Chihuahua.

I didn't see one small dog in my two days in Chihuahua. Two days was how long I had to wait until catching a train heading 418 miles/627km southwards to Los Mochis. The train was named El Chepe. Also known as the Copper Canyon Train.

Nestled in the Sierra Madre Range, Copper Canyon is actually several large canyons. Narrower and deeper, Copper Canyon is four times larger than America's Grand Canyon. This huge rugged territory of canyons and ridges covers up to twenty-five thousand square miles.

The Sierra Madre has a vast history of battle and discord from martyred Jesuits to Pancho Villa's army. It is also the homelands of the Tarahumara natives or self-called Rarámuri.

One of the largest indigenous tribes in North America with a population of one hundred thousand, most Rarámuri choose to live in the 'Las Barrancas' – the Sierra Madre's deep gorges. They also liked to run, a lot.

Narrow trails of dust and rubble ran parallel with Copper Canyon railway tracks. These were the trails of the Tarahumara Indians who are known to run up to one hundred miles barefoot in a day. I saw one running Tarahumara on my train journey south, his white skirt, red shirt and sleek black bobbed hair a blur as we passed each other in different directions.

I never made it to Los Mochis. Leaving the train all I remember about the town arrived in was a bar with nicotine stained sea bream walls and a TV showing Mike Tyson box his way to victory again.

Ready to return to America my journey northwards began.

Staying in small roadside hotels at night and travelling by local bus by day, I didn't retrace my steps taken southwards. Now I travelled to the Arizona border and its notorious Mexican border town of Nogales.

I was the only westerner boarding the last bus of my journey to the US border one morning. This bus would see me to Arizona that evening - a good ten hours away.

My fellow passengers practiced their English with me. I was happy for the company, feeling some comfort with these strangers when our bus came to a halt two hours from the American border.

A moustached police man with customary open shirt and mirrored sunglasses boarded. He made a beeline for me.

Handing over my passport to his grunt and receiving it back after his scrutiny he walked to the front of the bus. He turned to face all passengers and shouted his orders. I didn't understand his words.

"All men must get off the bus," the man sitting beside me said.

I settled back in my seat.

"You as well," the man smiled, aware my thoughts lay in - surely the police can't possibly mean me, I'm English.

I followed the aisle filled with men out into the desert surrounding a sandy highway. Twelve men dressed in black army fatigues from head to toe stood in a line, automatic rifles at the ready.

Told to get our bags from the bus's luggage hold, myself and the rest of the men on the bus stood in a line with our bags at our feet.

I looked to my backpack and then to those with rifles as they eyed us all and our bags.

After ten minutes we were released without a word. With bags put back in the hold and returning to our seats our bus revived its journey to America. I was given a can of coke by a passenger on returning to my seat. I'm sure he saw I needed some sugar.

I was told the stop was a routine occurrence. An unknown army looking for smuggled goods - people as well as drugs.

As night fell and with the US border just half an hour away I searched through my day bag again. The green immigration card stapled into my passport on my arrival from England into Miami was gone. After another frantic search it was no-where to be found.

That last thirty minutes on Mexican soil was as intimidating as encountering a dozen gun wielding soldiers.

I joined the line of those waiting to get into America. It got to my turn. I looked to the US immigration officer stood before me.

"I've lost my green paper," I held my passport open to him, pointing to the staple that had once held it in place.

The immigration officer stared back.

My journey had begun in Miami. From there I had travelled by train to New Orleans and into Texas. My intentions to travel onwards from Arizona to Los Angeles then north to Seattle now seemed in jeopardy.

I wondered what I would do. Would I go back into Mexico and try and find another way out? Would I have to stay in Mexico, forever?

I looked to the one who would either grant me entry or send me back to where I had come from.

The immigration man continued his stare.

"That's ok," he eventually said with a smile.

He reached into a drawer.

"You'll have to have a new one," he handed me a new green immigration card to fill in.

Chapter Fourteen

CHINA

Liberty and a First Novel

Hong Kong International Airport
Hong Kong
China
2005

Boarding a shuttle train at Hong Kong International Airport I looked out onto a country never visited before.

Four months earlier I had been in a liberation army camp under a blazing Burmese sun. Now I travelled alone with my backpack to Hong Kong's island of Kowloon.

Leaving Thailand a month after my excursion into war photography a return to England saw me try to settle. I lasted three months. Now I had a new plan. To travel around China writing my first novel.

China's mainland beckoned after a couple of days in Hong Kong. My journey began with a two hour train ride north to the city of Guangzhou - home to Peking duck and once a main port of the maritime Silk Road.

Guangzhou seemed a good enough starting point for what I

supposed a three month exploration of the country.

Guangzhou appeared little different to the western world. Young American couples walked the city's streets and parks, each with a Chinese baby in the pram pushed so eagerly. I later learnt that Guangzhou was where western couples wanting to adopt came - a few months stay in China a mandatory rule if to return home with an adopted baby boy or girl.

Opting to travel by bus I left Guangzhou and headed northwest for the town of Yangshuo.

Sitting on the banks of the Li River where fishermen use cormorants to catch fish, Yangshuo is overlooked by the Karst mountain range, a collection of tall limestone towers which run eastwards across southern China and into the landscapes of Vietnam.

Yangshuo was where I truly began to write my book.

A fictional story incorporating my travels and mystical experiences met with along the way, I wrote my words by hand in school exercise books readily found in China, as were the many pens I went through also.

Every morning I would edit what had been written the day before. In the afternoon I would write new words, as would I most evenings if company was not to be found. Those days and nights of writing were a joy. Writing in hotel rooms, coffee shops and restaurants, my first book slowly evolved.

A week in Yangshuo flew by. Many of the expat community there were mountain climbers under the spell of Moon Hill and its fourteen climbing routes on its north-west side. A few miles outside Yangshuo and part of the Guilin Mountains, Moon Hill's name derives from the wide semicircle hole through the hill.

I left Moon Hill to the professionals, having developed a fear of heights two years earlier in Pokhara, Nepal, when a paraglider I was harnessed to decided on breaking his personal altitude record, high above the Annapurna Range's sacred Fish Tail Mountain.

My travels continued and I headed northwest once more. A fourteen hour bus journey lay ahead to reach the city of Chengdu. I chose to split the journey into two.

Staying somewhere between Yangshuo and Chengdu for one night the hotel's restaurant had waitresses dressed as cheerleaders. Each one pushed a hostess trolley around the room with dishes of rice or chicken (neck and head attached) or beer and donuts.

Another seven hour bus ride saw me to Chengdu. It was during that bus ride that I touched upon sentiments met with only twice before - first in Paris, second on a train headed for Boston.

Sitting at the back of that bus to Chengdu, my backpack at my feet, I looked through the window's lines of silver rain drops and to the greenery beyond. All I had was me, a pack of smokes and my MP3 player. I had all I needed. I didn't know where I was, nor did anyone else I knew.

An absolute freedom surrounded me in that moment. If only fleeting, liberty had left her mark. Now I was really travelling. Now I was totally free. Free from constraints made in a hometown which seemed a million miles away. Although I was moving from place to place I felt more settled than ever before. I was content. I was happy.

My bus eventually delivered me to Chengdu.

Home of China's pandas, this small Chinese city of sixteen million was also a gateway to Tibet. A flight was needed to get to Lhasa, Tibet's capital – this was 2005 and it would be another year until the railway from Chengdu to Lhasa opened.

Flying into Tibet and staying for ten days I returned to Chengdu. There I met a friend and together we travelled three hours to the city of Chongqing, a place where some of the population walk round in silk pyjamas all day.

Staying one night in Chongqing we boarded a boat to take us downstream along the world's third longest river – The Yangtze.

Taking three days to sail through China's famed Three Gorges our boat passed by riverside empty villages, residents of which had been re-settled inland by the Chinese government, in sight of former homesteads being flooded to make way for hydroelectric plants.

Hillside temples and shrines lined our way along the Yangtze. A 6am visit to one such hilltop temple was made - only when an over eager tour guide continued to knock on a cabin door where two tired passengers tried to hide.

Docking in Wuhan, a one and a half hour flight was made to Xian, home of the Terracotta Warriors. From there another flight saw us to Beijing.

A duel hangover brought a stop to an intended visit to China's Great Wall. Legend says that if you see the Great Wall of China, then you shall return to China once more. I guessed I would see it from the plane to be taken to Shanghai. I didn't. It was cloudy. So I never got to go back to China. I can't go now anyway after working with a government in exile in an unknown future nine years away.

With two days in Shanghai my friend left for Australia. We would meet again three months later for a week in Bangkok and on one of Thailand's isles.

Saying our goodbyes I took a taxi back to Shanghai. I realised I had seen China in ten days. Now my book took prominence.

With no writing for the last ten days, my confidence was boosted when my friend had read a few early chapters - telling me they enjoyed my writing.

I headed south by train to the lakeside city of Hangzhou. Beside the waters of West Lake I would write for the next seven months.

A laptop was bought, yet still I wrote my story paper and pen. The only change now was my written words of the day were typed up in the evening and saved onto hard disk.

Finding a single room in a hostel on the banks of Hangzhou's celebrated lake I would walk northwards along its eastern side beneath lakeside willow trees. About half way up I would enter a regular coffee shop and write earnestly throughout the day.

Often the sun would be setting on my way home. On those evenings I would stop at the small pagoda at West Lake's south eastern corner, to watch a glowing orange sun disappear behind the lake I now lived beside.

The first draft of the book that had been written across China and Tibet was now complete and I left a much favoured lake. I travelled onwards with the one whose dark brown eyes became featured in my book. Together we journeyed to Sanya, a Chinese island just off Vietnam's coastline. From there it was a trip to Macau, then a flight to the white sands of Boracay Island in The Philippines.

Our farewells came in Bangkok. They to Australia, me to India for the second, third and final polish of my novel, but I was in no way alone. The characters within my book still accompanied me on my journey through these Asian countries.

Travelling from India's western beaches of Goa to the Himalayan reaches of Dharamsala, I found a home in McLeod Ganj. A place which would play a big part in my life for years to come.

It was there overlooking the rooftops of His Holiness the 14th Dalai Lama's place of residence that I completed my first novel. Its name? - Subway of Light.

Chapter Fifteen

INDIA

A Portuguese Legacy

Anjuna
Goa
India
December 2015

Sitting beneath swaying palm trees and on cliff tops overlooking the Arabian Sea, Catholic chapels and churches can be found throughout India's western state of Goa. Each one portrays a legacy left behind by the Portuguese.

When Vasco da Gama first stepped onto India's shores in 1498, he brought with him the Catholicism that still remains in Goa today.

Establishing a Portuguese colony in Goa in the early 16th century, these settlers in a new world so unlike their own began to construct churches and chapels to appease their want to serve God in the eyes of the Roman Catholic Church.

Some five hundred years later it was I who walked these holy grounds, camera at my side.

Arriving in India after leaving Nepal for visa requirements (via a week in Bangkok and two in Cambodia), Goa's hot weather and easy way of life was a much welcomed respite. The previous eight months had seen me experiencing and photographing Nepal's devastating earthquake's as well as the slow recovery of a country.

My new temporary home was a hotel stayed in a decade earlier in the coastal village of Anjuna. Although the hotel was now occupied entirely by Russians, the hotel pool was the main draw.

Now I needed a new project.

On my journey from Goa's airport to Anjuna, I had passed by the occasional church, chapel, and roadside shrine where crucifixes are garnished with rings of marigolds. These places of worship were no different than what can be found throughout Europe.

This would be my new project - these holy places looking so out of place amid sandy beaches, palm trees and the occasional monkey. This would be what I would photograph.

A scooter was hired and with my camera hanging around my neck I explored Goa in search of de Gama's mark on Asian soil.

Those first Portuguese settlers had followed the guidelines of classic Catholic architecture from their homelands. New structures of bell towers and steep white washed walls soon dominated a Goan landscape of coconut trees and rice fields. It would not be until the middle of the 20th century that Portugal lost all governing power in India.

Portugal's heritage is still much in evidence today. Indian nationals are either born into the faith or are converted. Catholicism in Goa is often practiced in the very places of worship established centuries earlier by the Portuguese.

I first took photos of Anjuna's own Catholic influence. Holy Cross Chapel was ideal - its white washed walls with edges of Mediterranean blue were stark in contrast to a palm tree backdrop.

On Anjuna's beachfront, 17th century St. Anthony's Chapel also commanded attention – a bell tower standing atop the chapel's three grey stone tiers as monsoon clouds held prominence above.

The towns on Goa's coastline were toured in shorts and t-shirt on a red scooter.

From the hippy enclave of Arombol in Goa's north down to Panaji in the state's centre, each destination brought a find of Catholic spaces searched for.

Photographs were taken in the towns of Vagator, Mapusa and Assagao, each place capturing the contrasts of different continents.

After five days photographing Catholic spaces found, my final church lay just a few short miles from my Anjuna base. The Church of St. Cajetan – patron saint of good fortune.

The largest church discovered on my self-styled Goan tour came with the freedom of being allowed to explore throughout these huge sacred grounds. Permission was given not by a resident priest, but by workmen repainting the church's tall white stone walls.

The church was immaculately kept and you could have been in any European place of worship. Not a soul was present, only I as I entered through St. Cajetan's aged wooden doors.

Goa's building heat was banished on my first footstep onto the church's rust coloured tiles. It was the first time experiencing the cold for a while.

Looking up to the high ceiling, halfway up a green painted balcony ran around where the congregation would sit taking mass below. As had their forefathers before them.

I walked down the aisle to the church's altar along a worn red carpet flanked on either side by long varnished pews.

Behind the church's alter ornate gold reliefs depicted stories from the bible. All were overlooked by a painted figure whom I supposed to be St. Cajetan himself.

Beside those holy depictions was an open doorway. A spiral staircase lay within.

Climbing those steps a further coolness surround me due to the cold brick walls I ascended between.

The staircase's first opening led to the green painted balcony high above a vacant congregation. This allowed a view of all the church's finery and ornate ceiling décor. Taking a few photographs I reentered the stairway and climbed up its steep curved steps once more.

A second opening led to a dimly lit room. I stayed on the stairs. Something held my curiosity back.

Staring into the room it felt colder than a stairway climbed.

Through windows covered with aged yellow newspaper shafts of light broke through several torn pages. That mediocre light illuminated a series of broken floorboards covered in years of dust. This was not the only reason for my apprehension.

The peace my camera usually gave escaped me. A feeling of dread replaced my usual stillness. There was something not right about the room. Eeriness sounded off each of its four walls of flaking plaster.

I looked up.

One corner of the ceiling was moving. I looked closer. Like tiny waves on a disturbed pond, several small black bats hung down, their dark leathery wings in constant slight flutter.

Telling myself I had taken enough photographs for the day, I went down St. Cajetan's steps much quicker than I had up them.

Chapter Sixteen

Cambodia

Monks, Skulls and Monsoons

Siem Reap
Cambodia
2015

Taking control of the country in 1975 the tyrant Pol Pot led Cambodia's Communist regime, better known as the Khmer Rouge.

A Marxist–Leninist and Khmer nationalist, Pol Pot's ideology stated that a country's traditions and culture must be completely destroyed in order for a new revolutionary society to replace it. Pol Pot's initiation of Year Zero gave his Democratic Kampuchea that new beginning.

This new beginning oversaw the execution of intellectuals, teachers, and artists. A time when being caught wearing glasses or carrying a book on the streets of Phnom Penh meant immediate death in the capital's Killing Fields, where pathways embedded with victim's bones and fragments of torn clothing remain to this day.

Pol Pot's regime was not just in Cambodia's south.

Far from the capital's Killing Fields, Cambodia's northern city of Siem Reap also has its memorial to those who perished under the command of the Khmer Rouge.

Beside the river banks cutting through the town, the Buddhist temple of Wat Thmei is within an area which once served as one of Siem Reap's own Killing Fields during the Khmer Rouge's time.

In Pol Pot's reign the temple served as a prison where innocent Cambodians were tortured until confessing to crimes they had not committed. They were then killed and buried near Wat Thmei's temple grounds.

A monastery and place of worship once more, Wat Thmei has two memorials for those who fell under the Khmer Rouge. A red painted pagoda and a golden pagoda each with tall glass walls. Pol Pot's victims fill each stupa, their bones and skulls exhumed and put on display.

With an exhibition of photographs depicting the atrocities committed, these memorials provide an unsettling reminder for Siem Reap's community of genocidal events between 1975 and 1979.

Taking advantage of a Cambodian early evening golden hour light I entered Wat Thmei's grounds. The pagodas I had come to photograph were half full.

Several monks in orange robes gathered around and inside the red and gold memorials. They were making their twice yearly duty of dusting the bones within.

Wat Thmei's monks ignored my presence as I left my footwear behind and stepped barefoot up to the golden pagoda.

Two young monks lifted a makeshift stretcher of orange robes from the pagoda. They carried within that bowing stretcher a variety of ribs, thighs and arm bones.

Placing them down they then carefully dusted each tan stained bone of the innocent.

The red memorial also gained the respectful attentions of Wat Thmei's residents. Each monk handled the display of countless skulls with care, dusting each one before placing it back - producing a window display of hollow eye sockets and a bared top row of teeth.

I took a photo of one monk dusting each skull with care. He looked to me as I pressed the shutter, his eyes wide above a surgical facemask - his shaved scalp merging into a backdrop of skulls.

There would be one more photo taken that day which summed up the enormity of the Cambodian genocide. This was seen in the features of Thmei's elderly chief monk.

Overseeing the cleaning operation he leant one hand on the red memorial. In a brief moment he looked to the skulls now free from six months of dust. His expression was one of sorrow combined with disbelief. Disbelief his country had acted such a way in a not so distant past.

Raindrops began to dot the temple courtyard. Previous brisk winds rattling through Wat Thmei signalled an upcoming downpour.

Temple dogs pulled themselves from their slumber. They knew of the rains to come as much as their monk landlords.

Dogs are always allowed to roam free throughout South East Asia's temples. Allowed because all monks remember their teacher's words when they were once a novice – that if you don't learn your prayers correctly, you will come back as a temple dog in the next lifetime.

In a split second the rains began to fall. This is how it is with monsoons. A sudden deluge after a day's building heat. A rainfall which would stop as abruptly as it had started, with only a cooler feel to the evening to show of its once wet presence.

The monsoons have always been a part of the South East Asia I know.

A first experiencing of such rains came when arriving in Chiang Mai, Thailand, for the first time. Unbeknown to me then I would see three other monsoons there – Chiang Mai being a place where an intended ten day visit evolved into a three year stay.

Bangkok's rainy season has been experienced many times also, where warm rain is delivered across the city in an early evening torrent.

Cambodia fared no different in ways of monsoon seasons. This would be when a much favoured swim would take place.

Hotel pools would become deserted when the rains struck, tourists fearing the occasional thunderclap from above. This would leave a pool free from others and as warm as a hot shower.

Diving into a solitary pool the thrashing noise of rain against swimming pool surface would disappear. Only a muted swish entered the pool when swimming a length beneath the water.

Breaching the surface for breath I would watch raindrops dance around me as they fell and bounced back up like a million pins.

As the rains ceased and the evening took on a cooler air Siem Reap's flood ridden streets began to clear. Its temporary waters would subside within the hour.

All that would be left now was a night's sleep accompanied by the call of a thousand bullfrogs, each creature's loud croak prompted by a monsoon's touch.

Chapter Seventeen

Tibet

Yak Butter Tea and a Sacred Lake

Lhasa
Tibet
2005

After travelling north along China's western border my arrival at the city of Chengdu provided me with a journey into Tibet.

The only realistic way to reach Tibet's capital Lhasa was by flight. In 2005 the train which today can transport you from Chengdu to Lhasa was a year off completion.

A single traveller was not permitted to enter Tibet alone. Only groups of five or more were allowed, and then at least three had to be of different nationality. A Chinese travel agent added me to a group of other single foreign travellers also keen to see Tibet for themselves.

On the flight to Lhasa one thought lay in each tourist's mind - the problem of altitude on those with no experience of thin air before. Flying into Lhasa's high altitude of 11,990 feet/3,656 metres gave the body no time to acclimatise.

The only way to discover if you were going to get altitude sickness was to be there. If you were to suffer from being at such a height you had less than twenty-four hours in which to leave Tibet for lower ground, or else the results were often fatal.

Landing in Lhasa not one of us succumbed to altitude. Although climbing stairs did produce light headedness. Also I discovered when unpacking that my toothpaste tube had exploded in my toiletry bag, and the packet of crisps I had stowed away with me now resembled an inflatable cushion. These effects of high altitude only added to the realisation that I truly was in a foreign land.

On my arrival to the Tibetan capital I ventured into Lhasa's Barkhor Square. It was a walk back in time. The one kilometre square heart of Lhasa's Tibetan community remained as it had for centuries.

Market stall traders sold a variety of meats with goat heads and legs hung from red stained hooks - fur and hoof remaining. Beside them wicker baskets filled with yak spun yarn took place next to trays of fresh and dried herbs brought in from surrounding hillsides.

A maze of lanes and alleyways criss-crossed the square between grey stone buildings - homes and restaurants for those who considered this setting a last bastion of a once true Lhasa.

Following the Chinese invasion into Tibet one early October day in 1950, Tibet has suffered from the continual wish of the Chinese government to dilute the Tibetan bloodline and assimilate the Tibetan people into its own culture.

His Holiness the 14th Dalai Lama escaped Tibet at the age of twenty-three in the spring of 1959. Leaving Potala Palace disguised as a soldier, His Holiness met with a group of Buddhist monks from Gyuto monastery and a handful of Tibetan resistance fighters 37 miles/60km outside Lhasa. What followed was a hazardous two week trek over the Himalayas and into India. His Holiness was then allowed by the Indian government to live and form a Tibetan government in exile in India's northern town of Dharamsala.

Tibet's recent turbulent history was what made Barkhor Square so unique. The Chinese government had promised the Tibetan people Barkhor would remain as it had always been. That there would be no Chinese influence within that hallowed one square kilometre. A promise they had seemed to have kept in 2005.

Not bringing my digital camera with me to China I bought a camera. A disposable one. I was back to using film once more. Now I had only thirty-six shots to capture all around me, not the usual hundreds a digital camera allowed before saving and deleting, giving an infinite amount of photographs at my disposal.

One noticeable thing about this restriction is a slowing down in activity. Each shot was now carefully chosen.

It was a good exercise. It taught patience and precision. Even now with my digital camera I sometimes tell myself I only have thirty-six precious shots. It slows you down - allowing mindfulness to come forth into your picture taking.

I was to find out in years to come that photographs taken on that small disposable camera of Barkhor's lanes and alleys documented a community and setting slowly becoming lost to the world. Those photos taken of Lhasa in 2005 would be shown to an audience thirteen years later in 2018, when giving a talk for Free Tibet in London, UK.

Using film once more came with another factor. Developing.

I found somewhere to develop my film opposite my next destination, His Holiness' former home Potala Place. Told the photos would take an hour I found a bench overlooking Potala.

It began to rain.

Across from me a large sign hung above a doorway. It just said Tea. Making my way to the building in hope they had coffee I entered into another world again.

There must have been over two hundred monks sitting in a vast room of benches and tables. A sea of burgundy robes capped by crops of black hair - all under a constant hum of Tibetan chatter. That chatter died down as I walked into the room.

Spying the only seat free was in the middle of the room I sat down there. A small cup of yak butter tea was placed before me.

The monks went back to their talking. That was except one opposite me. He smiled and raised his cup to me in cheers. Following his actions I took a sip. It was so hot I thought they had given me lava. On top of that it tasted awful. Not wanting to be rude I smiled and said it was delicious. That monk saw straight through me and laughed.

Embarrassed, I reached into my bag and pulled out my notepad and pen. I was now five chapters through my hand written novel.

Aware the monk opposite watched my every move with great curiosity I began to write. I only got a quarter down the page when my pad and pen were taken from me. The monk began to write below my words. After writing two lines he handed my notepad back and smiled once more.

Looking to those two lines of Tibetan script I tried to ask him what it said. He waved his hand indicating he spoke no English.

I continued to write my story below the monk's words.

That piece of paper has been with me ever since. I have yet to get it translated. Maybe I will one day, but I worry it may take the magic out of a such a nice memory.

Continuing to document a fading Tibet on film with more disposable cameras I visited one of Tibet's four sacred lakes.

The high altitude played heavy on me standing on the lapping shores of Namsto Lake, a body of water so large its 740 miles^2/1,920 km^2 surface has its own tidal system.

At 15,479 feet/4,718 metres above sea level it began to be difficult to walk a few steps without stopping and catching my breath - and so I rode on the back of a saddled yak to the minibus waiting to return me to Lhasa for my final few days there.

Chapter Eighteen

Jordan

A Walk to The Rose City

Petra
Jordan
February 2011

Arriving in Egypt three days earlier I found myself on a bus trip to Petra in Jordan's southwestern desert landscape.

My planned intention to visit Egypt was not to visit another country to see the red stone temples seen in movies as a child. I was making my way to Cairo. It was there in the Egyptian capital that the Arab Spring was in full flow. I had flown from England to capture the demonstrations first hand with my camera.

Flying into a military airport in the north eastern corner of the country, there were only a handful of other foreign guests in my hotel in the tourist complex of Taba Heights. The Arab Spring uprising was starting to spread across North Africa and into the Middle East. This had made holiday makers wary of visiting such volatile places.

Due to this lack of visitors I was upgraded to a suite room. From my bed I could see Taba Heights' Egyptian seafront, Saudi Arabia stretching out across the Gulf of Aqaba, Jordan's border point, and if

I leaned to the left Israel's border was just about visible too. In fact Israel's border with Egypt was so close the bus from the airport had let someone off there just before arriving to my hotel.

Unsure as what to find in Cairo, I put thoughts of photographing the heated demonstrations to be found in Tahrir Square aside. Now I wanted to see Petra.

Dating back to 300BC, Petra was once the capital of the Nabatean Kingdom. Used for shelter by nomadic shepherds for several centuries, Petra was discovered again by Swiss explorer Johann Ludwig Burckhardt in 1812.

Accessed only by an ever narrowing and twisting canyon trail, Petra is a collection of tombs and temples carved into cliffs of pink and red sandstone.

A boat trip from Taba to the Jordanian border took a half hour, Jordan's immigration just twenty minutes. A six hour bus journey brought myself and a group of twenty other tourists to the beginning of a four mile walk to Petra. Tensions were high at the mouth of that pathway.

Waiting to begin our journey a local man approached me. He raised an imaginary machine gun and placed at least a dozen imaginary bullets in my torso.

"American," he snarled, complete with a spit of disgust on the floor between us.

"English," I told him.

One of the two security guards assigned to our group walked over.

"American," the local barked again. With another spit onto his own country's soil he was gone – and I took my NY baseball cap off.

The walk with the group was arduous. Headed by a security guard at the front and one at the rear, some members of the group insisted on taking photographs of everything we passed.

All the stopping and starting made me all the more keen to see Petra's temples, these sandstone shrines of Sinbad and Indiana Jones etched into a once younger mind.

I broke away from the group. Our guide was too occupied with those holding everyone back to care. Although his warning of be careful was heeded.

With the group far behind a pathway once flanked by open space began to narrow. Just before entering between tall sandstone walls a group of local horsemen stood. They eyed the lone westerner away from his group.

My nod hello met with blank stares and I hurried my step on hearing 'American,' muttered again that day. This was followed by what seems a customary spit onto dry parched land.

Walking onwards the path narrowed more until tall sandstone walls of varying coloured stripes replaced Jordan's arid backdrop.

Looking back I saw my group were nearing. I pushed forwards, overwhelmed by my want to walk through the end of this narrow path known as Al Siq, and into Petra's wide open space.

Every blind turn the path made raised my expectation that this was the opening into Petra. Halfway through those twists and turns between high sandstone walls the sound of hooves echoed towards me. After taking a photo of the galloping horse pulling a swaying carriage behind it I jumped aside. Pushing myself against cool sandstone it was evident the driver was not going to stop for some random American tourist.

Those blind turns went on for nearly one mile. Each time my expectations rose. My anticipations were reached when at last rounding a corner and seeing what lay beyond the end of my path. I took one photo - sandstone walls framing an opening revealing Petra's most famous structure, The Treasury, a lone camel's head and neck completing the composition.

Leaving the path behind and stepping out into warm sunlight I looked around. I was the only person there, except that was for a collection of camels and their owners further along Petra's walls. For now I mostly had Petra's iconic temple to myself.

I stared up at the 148 feet/45 metre high Al Khazneh, a temple with an ornate Greek style façade carved into the cliffside.

Believed to be the Nabatean King Aretas IV's mausoleum and dating back to the 1st century BC, Al Khazneh's name *The Treasury* comes from the early nineteen hundreds when Bedouins visiting Petra believed it contained ancient treasures of long passed Pharaohs and kings.

Walking forward and standing at the foot of Al Khazneh, I looked to its columns holding the structure up. It was hard to grasp that this was not a building, but a frontage expertly sculptured into pink sandstone cliff walls, earning its nickname of *The Rose City*.

The rest of my group entered Petra and the city was no longer my own – a unique moment of solitude for which an Arab Spring was to be blamed/commended.

With hours spent exploring Petra's other temples and tombs an uphill climb was made to return to an awaiting bus ready to carry all back into Egypt. This time I remained with the group in an approaching dusk light.

Returning to my Egyptian hotel late that night I prepared for my journey west across the country to Cairo the next day.

With a bus ticket to the capital bought the previous day and a camera bag packed and at the ready, I was prepared to face Cairo's Arab Spring demonstrations. Or at least I thought I was.

Chapter Nineteen

Egypt

An Arab Spring, a Taxi and a Sphinx

Cairo
Egypt
February 2011

Leaving the comfort of a hotel suite, a pool and general safety, I handed over my one way ticket to Cairo as I boarded a direct bus from Taba to the capital.

The Arab Spring demonstrations in Cairo lay 256 miles/413km away. It was going to be a long journey. As was usual I was the only westerner on the bus.

My reason for being in Egypt was to go to Cairo and photograph the emerging Arab Spring protests in Tahrir Square - also known as *Martyr Square*.

Present for Bangkok's government and military crackdown in 2009 (as I would be again in 2014), I saw a similar opportunity to document history again. I bought a flight from the UK to Taba Heights in northeastern Egypt.

After staying in Taba Heights in a near empty hotel and visiting Jordan's Petra I made my way to Cairo.

I had always wanted to go to the Egyptian capital. My granddad had served there during World War II. A driver for Majors and Generals, he would transport them across the city from venue to venue in a sleek black Bentley.

Looking out onto barren fields passing by my window I wondered if the same streets he had driven through and I was to walk were as unsafe as I thought they were going to be.

After hours of driving the bus pulled up at an army checkpoint on Cairo's edge. All passengers were told to get off. We were lined up against the bus and looked over by the soldiers present.

Being the only westerner on the bus prompted the same confused stares encountered in Mexico by another army - a foreigner en route to what was hoped to be the beginnings of change throughout the Arab communities of North Africa and the Middle East.

One of the soldiers took my passport. He looked to me and handed it back, waving his hand to get back on the bus with a shake of his head.

Eventually arriving at Cairo's main bus station I found a taxi and climbed into the back. Telling the driver the hotel I planned to go to he turned to me.

"That hotel has burnt down," he said

In my years of travelling experience I have met no end of taxi drivers from across the world who received commissions for every tourist diverted to favoured hotels.

"Just take me to that hotel", I said, tired and wanting a shower.

"It burnt down last night. I will take you to my brother's hotel. It's very nice."

"Please, just take me where I want to go."

He gave a shrug and began to drive.

Twenty minutes later the taxi came to a stop.

"Your hotel," the driver pointed to the rubble and smouldering shell of a building beside us.

"Take me to your brother's hotel," I said.

He did without another word.

After settling into the taxi driver's brother's hotel I walked out into late evening Cairo towards Tahrir Square.

The protests against the government had seen an influx of army personnel, complete with tanks at their disposal. Demonstrations had begun in Cairo on the 25th January 2011.

Activists had called for an uprising in their own country to protest against poverty and government corruption. Their main demonstrations were against the presidential rule of Hosni Mubarak who had been in power for the last three decades.

Only days before my arrival these demonstrations had seen the army firing gunshots into the air to disperse thousands of protesters gathered in the square.

On my approach to Tahrir I saw the tanks waiting for instruction on the square's perimeter surrounding those calling for their president's resignation.

My senses told me not to walk into those crowds. I didn't. Paying heed to my intuitions I instead walked around the square. After an hour or two I realised this was a different setting from those used to in South East Asia. I made my way back to my hotel.

The next morning I summed up the situation and decided against visiting Tahrir Square again. Instead I choose to walk the area around my hotel. Surely there would be a group of soldiers and a spare tank somewhere on the streets. I soon found what I was looking for.

Across from my hotel a tank was adorned by two armed soldiers.

Raising my camera I tried to capture the scene. Every time either a car passed by or I was scuppered by a constant flow of people.

Not wanting to seem suspicious and trying again and again to take my photo bloody mindedness came into play. After twenty minutes I just walked across the street, stood in front of the tank and its soldiers and took the photo. Lowering my camera I smiled at them.

There were no smiles in return and my instincts took hold again.

Walking briskly away I turned the corner onto another street and quickened my pace. I saw a cake shop and darted inside. Within seconds the two soldiers ran past the doorway of my hiding place leaving me unseen and surrounded by cakes. I bought two and ate them in the shop. I made each one last, so giving me more time to keep out of sight, much to the confusion of the cake shop owner behind the counter.

On returning to my hotel I booked a flight home in two days' time. As I was here I thought I had better see the pyramids. I had no interest in attempting to photograph the troubles within the city anymore. This really was a very different place to the Asia I felt so comfortable in.

The pyramids were as spectacular as I had imagined.

Maybe this was due to only me and a smattering of Chinese tourists having the whole setting to ourselves. There was no-one in sight when walking around the base of Cairo's Great Pyramid.

Standing before the Sphinx I found myself amid a group of those Chinese tourists. Raising my camera in unison with them I began to click away.

Chapter Twenty

Japan

A Tokyo Respite

Tokyo
Japan
December 2016

I was in Asia, but I wasn't. This was Tokyo's welcome.

Although surrounded by a sense of the Asian cities I knew so well, a silence settled over neon lit streets, ancient temple and shrine.

This combination of the traditional and the new found within Tokyo's metropolis provided a cityscape like no other. Japan's capital embraced a fusion of time periods from both eras, merging effortlessly and with no conflict at all.

Tokyo's subway system runs everywhere beneath the city. I explored everywhere with ease taking subway trains in all directions across the capital.

After over a year photographing Nepal's earthquake and its recovery I was ready to capture images with a softer touch. Japan seemed ideal to do so.

In a first venture out with my camera I arrived in the Shibuya district of Harajuku.

Across the road from Harajuku station is the entrance to Takeshita Street, Tokyo's popular walkway selling the latest Japanese fashions. Behind the station Yoyogi Park beckoned visitors to walk between its one hundred thousand trees taken from all regions of Japan.

Tokyo's subtle silence multiplied within the forested area of Yoyogi Park, a neat stone pathway leading all to walk beneath tall wooden Torii gates towards the sacred grounds of Meiji Shrine.

A Shinto shrine dedicated to the deified spirits of Emperor Meiji and his wife Empress Shōken, Meiji Shrine is a popular setting for weddings. A wedding ceremony had begun as I walked into the Meiji's holy grounds.

Two families soon to be joined together stood in two lines waiting to enter Meiji Shrine. Bride and groom stood side by side. Each one headed their family behind them.

Both standing in patience, the groom's traditional black silk male kimono enriched his bride's traditional attire of pure white, signifying Japan's association with the colour of purity.

The bride's outfit was completed by a wataboshi - a large oval hood worn to conceal her features from everyone present except her husband to be.

Another venture lay four subway stops from Harajuku. Tokyo's famous pedestrian 'scramble' crossing of Shibuya.

With a population nearing half a million the special ward of Shibuya is one of Tokyo's main shopping districts.

Surrounded by neon lights and beneath the gaze of huge video screens, Shibuya is home to the world's busiest intersection. At peak times over one thousand people cross together from all directions. Like a giant shoal of fish not a soul touches as they rush across Shibuya's pedestrian crossings.

For another five days I set out to capture the city with my camera.

One place visited was in the near centre of the city where the 16th century Zōjō-ji Temple stands beneath the red and white stripes of Tokyo Tower.

The head temple of the Kanto Region's Japanese Buddhist branch of the Jodo sect, Zōjō-Ji was first constructed in 1393 and moved to its present location in 1598. Sitting beside Tokyo Tower the temple is visited daily by devotees from across Japan.

To the north of the city is Tokyo's Ueno Park. Its tranquil lakes are lined with cherry blossom trees, each waiting for the last days of March, when their displays of pink blossom attracts over ten million visitors a year to witness the heights of Hanami (Japan's springtime cherry blossom season).

Filled with museums, temples and shrines, Ueno Park's three hundred acre grounds are located in the Ueno district of Tokyo.

Established in 1873 on land formerly owned by the temple of Kan'ei-Ji, the park's style is fashioned by that of the early Meiji period.

Tokyo at night was a much different place than the peaceful gardens and parks of Yoyogi and Ueno.

Shinjuku's Kabukicho district is famous for its late-night entertainment of adult-oriented nightlife. Running from Shinjuku's main drag, lantern-lit alleys are crammed tight with small clubs, pubs, and late-night snack bars.

Shinjuku railway station hosts two million passengers a day, making it the biggest railway station in the world. To the north of this vast station is Shinjuku's Omoide Yokocho (memory lane) – also known as Yakitori Alley.

Small restaurants run the length of the one hundred metre or so Yakitori Alley. Each one lit by lanterns of whites, oranges and reds. These small restaurants provide up to four or five stools for customers to sit and eat their *yakitori* – bamboo skewered chicken seasoned with tare sauce or salt and grilled over a charcoal fire.

Away from Yakitori Alley, Shinjuku's skyscrapers tower above the Kabukicho district. Made to scale, Godzilla pokes his head over the side of one hotel and acts as one of the rooms.

Taking in all these sights brought a peace which had been a little lost over the previous year. It was not that I hadn't enjoyed my photography within the settings of volcanoes, slums and earthquakes. Then I had found a similar peace. Yet, Japan gave a much different personal harmony.

The calm found and experienced capturing Tokyo frame by frame gave relief to a much harder edge usually craved. Now my photography was purely for enjoyment, with Japan providing endless compositions for my lens as well as peace of mind.

I would leave Tokyo and travel south to Japan's former capital Kyoto, a journey by bullet train which took just two and a quarter hours to cover a total distance of 282 miles/454km.

With a week spent in Hiroshima, another bullet train was taken back to the capital. My return to Tokyo found me experiencing another earthquake - this time one of only 4.2 magnitude.

Spending Christmas in Tokyo I left for Thailand. Spending New Year's Eve in Bangkok, two weeks later I was celebrating my birthday in Kathmandu.

In this whirlwind of such contrasting countries the uniqueness of each capital city wins through.

Tokyo, Bangkok, Kathmandu. For me each place holds its own culture, its own traditions… its own enchantment.

Chapter Twenty-One

India

Pujas, Mandalas and Fireballs

Gyuto Tantric Monastery
Sidhbari
India
January 2016

I was back in McLeod Ganj. My American friend craved tea.

We would go to different places throughout McLeod sampling what teas were on offer. I stuck to black coffee each time, a strange role reversal between each country's national drink.

I met an Argentinian couple while hunting for said teas. They were documentary filmmakers travelling in India to promote their latest film about ayahuasca shamans. They had a new project here in McLeod Ganj.

Seeing my photographs they asked me to join that project. I accepted as soon as they told me they would be filming the nearby Gyuto Tantric Monastery.

With my American friend's departure I focused on what lay ahead, enjoying the thought of working with others as the three of us crammed ourselves and equipment into one of McLeod's small ramshackle taxi cabs, plummeting down twisting lanes until reaching flatter grounds of the Kangra Valley and Sidhbari - the village setting of Gyuto Monastery.

Gyuto Tantric Monastery is home to His Holiness the 17th Karmapa and the five hundred Buddhist monks who study there in Gyuto's monastic Buddhist university.

One of the main tantric universities of the Gelug tradition of Tibetan Buddhism, Gyuto was first established in Lhasa, Tibet, by Jetsun Kunga Dhondup in 1475.

Home to one thousand monks at the time of the Chinese invasion into Tibet, a group of Gyuto's monks escaped to India across the Himalayas with His Holiness the 14th Dalai Lama in the spring of 1959. These monks went on to initiate the Gyuto Monastery now found on the outskirts of Dharamsala today.

Famed for its unique overtone singing using a traditional Tibetan technique, this would not only be what we had come to document. Gyuto's three day annual puja (prayer meeting) for bringing peace and health across the world for the coming year was three days away. We had arrived at the start of their prayer ceremony preparations.

Walking between the monk's quarters of Tibetan design several sets of steps led us into Gyuto's courtyard. I took my first photo there as a monk in burgundy robes walked towards us in the distance.

Behind him stood the Karmapa Temple, its bright yellow walls complete with two sweeping red staircases leading from either side of its doors and down into the courtyard. All this was to a backdrop of Himalayan snow tipped mountain peaks beneath an Indian winter's bright blue sky. This would be where the puja was to be held. In this yellow temple inaugurated by His Holiness the 14th Dalai Lama in the autumn of 1998 - year of the firemouse in the Tibetan lunar calendar.

Climbing one of the red staircases I entered the Karmapa Temple.

Long rows of low red padded seats on either side of a wide aisle awaited Gyuto's monks. A small stage stood at the end of that aisle, behind which Buddha statues lined the temple's far wall. A huddle of monks sat at the temple's far right hand corner.

Each one knelt on the floor leaning over a near completed sand mandala. Each fragment of its circular design of Buddhist symbols were painstakingly laid down grain by grain by hand. This mandala would be swept away towards the end of the puja, signifying the impermanence of the physical and bringing a lesson of non-attachment to those who had laboured so hard over the display.

Meeting with Gyuto's head monks we were invited to document the preparations and eventual puja. We began the next day.

After another roller-coaster taxi ride to Gyuto the next morning we met with a new sight outside the Karmapa temple.

On the terrace atop its red staircases twenty or so monks sat before temple doors. Each one rolled out white balls of dough. A mixture of tsampa (Tibetan barley and water), they molded every piece into ceremonial shapes ready to be painted when dry.

These individual pieces would go on to become a human sized effigy topped by a large skull complete with darkened eyes and pearl white teeth. This was to be then set alight on prepared bonfires in the puja's closing ceremony as nighttime fell.

There were many preparations happening all around the temple.

Butter sculptures of characters from Buddhist scripture were made. Bowls of freezing iced water were placed in front of each sculpting monk. They dipped their hands into them frequently to stop warm fingertips melting their intricate offerings. Butter sculptures of lotus flowers and other elements of nature were made - all to be cast in awaiting bonfires yet to be lit. Another lesson in impermanence.

During those days of preparation there was a constant tending to a small fire in the middle of Gyuto's courtyard. Overseen by monks, above that small fire sat a sealed long brown clay waist high pot. As its contents of hot oil kept bubbling slathers of wet clay were placed around any appearing cracks which may release the boiling liquid.

This tending to the oil continued until the end of the puja. It was then I at last found out why such care was taken over its cooking.

The first day of the puja arrived. It began with the chants of Gyuto's monks.

Our team had been joined by a French lady. Together the four of us were allowed to sit quietly within the temple to listen to the religious prayers sung in deep toned chants.

As one monk began to chant another soon joined, then another and another until all those sat on red padded seating chanted in unison. Sound resonated off each temple hall wall, wrapping your whole body up in notes unheard of before - pressing down across ribcage and forehead. The chanting intensified and the temple became an unworldly combination of sound and holy fervor.

The following days of prayer and chants within the puja continued with a growing intensity. This strange environment only led me to enter into the temple on brief occasions.

Names of those passed were read out by the head monks and the completed sand mandala was swept away. A sight which was not for our eyes. This ritual was taken in silence behind aged Tibetan rugs held up high by novice monks living within the monastery.

Gyuto's ceremony was coming to an end. As dusk began on the puja's final night Tibetans living in McLeod Ganj and Dharamsala arrived to Gyuto's courtyard. They were here to see the annual closing rites performed by Gyuto's resident monks.

It started with the tsampa sculptured skull and its thin body being carried precariously down red temple steps by ten monks, all attempting to keep the effigy stable whilst trying not to trip over their robes. Their feat accomplished the goal now was to take it to bonfires which had started to smoulder to the left of the courtyard.

Ceremonial horns and drums sounded out across the grounds as dusk cast a purple light over those of the puja.

As night came the music faded and gathering crowds began to circle a constantly burning hot oil pot in the centre of the courtyard.

With the Argentinians filming I stood with a French photographer. Both of us were unaware as to what was to happen next.

Beneath a blackened sky, one monk who had tended the boiling oil for days stood before its hot clay container. The crowd edged back. They knew what was to unfold.

The monk sliced off the top of the pot and returned to his brothers at the edge of the crowd. Two long sticks extended out to the bubbling oil, one with a flame at its end, the other with a bowl of water attached. The first stick lit the oil. The second poured water onto those flames.

A fire ball of the brightest orange exploded and reached up high into the night sky.

As the crowd moved back I instinctively moved forward to get a better shot. I didn't know the oil was to be lit twice.

The heat was intense. As was the smell of the left eyebrow I had just lost and the burning plastic rim of my camera lens.

Chapter Twenty-Two

Bhutan

Holy Rites and Luxury Hotels

Paro
Bhutan
October 2014

18,000 feet/5,486 metre snowcapped mountain peaks flank the approach to Bhutan's main airport, classing it as one of the most dangerous approaches in the world.

With Paro's runway less than half the length of any other international airport's, only a handful of qualified pilots are authorised to land there. Night time landings are not permitted.

What makes Paro's decent so perilous is its runway. Out of sight until the final minute, skilled pilots have a small window to fly between the city's steep hillside homes at a forty-five degree angle before dropping onto the runway.

This was my entry into Bhutan one October morning, filled with expectations to what my camera would capture in 'The Land of The Thunder Dragon'.

My anticipations proved expensive.

The visa for Bhutan was $250 USD per day. Although that visa included a personal guide, a car and driver, all meals, and a stay in Bhutan's five star hotels each night, this extravagance was more than worth it. This was confirmed in the photographs taken throughout this private kingdom.

Met by my guide and driver at the airport at 8.00am, my four day tour of Bhutan began there and then.

First we were to travel to the city of Thimphu, an hour plus drive through countryside so different to any ever seen before.

Steep rock faced cliffs ran either side of the highway leading to Bhutan's capital. Those cliffs would wane at times to reveal forested hillsides and copper green rivers fed from towering waterfalls.

Bhutan's landscape ranges from subtropical plains in the south to northern sub-alpine mountains where snowcapped peaks can be found in excess of 23,000 feet/7,000 metres. With the mountain of Gangkhar Puensum recognised as the highest peak in Bhutan, it is said to be the highest unclimbed mountain in the world.

Travel to Bhutan is highly regulated. The government sees that only a limited number of tourists enter into Bhutan at any one time.

Under the policy of 'high value/low impact tourism' this minimises the impact on the country's environment and culture of Bhutan's population of below one million. These measures are taken so as not to become overwhelmed by mass tourism, as can be seen in South East Asia.

This gave travelling in Bhutan an added flavour. You really were a stranger in a strange land. With the added bonus that you were not surrounded by westerners.

Arriving in Thimphu saw to dropping my bags in my hotel for the night. My room overlooked the city streets - streets famed for having no traffic lights. In fact there was not one in the whole country. This is when I saw where my expensive visa was going. Even though I was excited for the coming day and the sights to be seen, I was equally keen to spend time in a hotel room of such luxury.

Our first stop was Thimphu's Memorial Stupa.

Also known as the Thimphu Chorten, The Memorial Stupa was built to represent the mind of The Buddha. It seemed I had arrived in the middle of a festival. Monks, nuns and devotees swarmed around the walled open space.

With a three story stupa elaborately decorated with gold leaf in the centre of the grounds, prayer flags spanned out in every direction above the heads of all from its domed rooftop.

I asked what festival this was.

"There is no festival, it is always like this. Every day," my guide replied.

In awe that this was a daily occasion I walked around those praying and meditating with my camera.

Most were willing to have their portrait taken. As were others happy for me to photograph them as they walked in a clockwise direction around the stupa, reciting mantras as they went and spinning hand held prayer wheels, the written prayers encased within them multiplying each prayer a thousand fold on every turn.

At the far corner of the stupa grounds rows of flat wooden plinths sat inches above the ground. Each one was the size to allow a human body to lay on completely. These plinths were for prostrations, a Buddhist practice where a devotee stands with hands held in prayer before bowing, kneeling down, and then stretching out on their front before returning to their original standing position. This is seen as one prostration. Viewed as a means of overcoming pride, this act of devotion often has a preliminary practice of completing 100,000 prostrations a year.

Watching Bhutanese Buddhists carryout their prostrations I recalled my time in Tibet. I had seen such rituals performed outside the doors of Lhasa's Potala Palace. Only there those prostrating moved forward one step at a time after carrying out three prostrations. Those I witnessed on their arrival to Potala were at the end of their journey having prostrated all the way from their home, sometimes at distances of thousands of miles. A journey that could take up to two years or more to complete.

I always felt honoured that I lay witness to the completion of such an arduous task. An unimaginable act of both physical and mental strength these devotees of Buddha had undertaken.

In Bhutan's capital I photographed those who showed their devotion to Buddha through physical worship, the way I had nine years earlier in Tibet. Only then in 2005 it had been with a disposable camera, not the two kilogram set up I held now, camera strap wrapped twice around my right wrist as always.

Our next stop was to the Tashichho Dzong Fortress Monastery on the banks of the Wang Chu River at the northern edge of the city.

Unbelievably high whitewashed walls rose up from a large grey slate courtyard within the monastery. The courtyard's emptiness was dismissed as a lone monk in burgundy robes walked across the scene.

Thankful for the Bhutanese government's restrictions towards tourists, this allowed for photographic compositions unheard of in another country's main attractions.

Walking through these grounds gave an insight into what it would be to live a monastic life beneath high wooden beamed and gold set rooftops.

As my first day closed, I at last made it to the hotel room. Showered and settled for the night I sank into the luxury around me.

Laying on the bed and finding a movie to watch my right eye closed. This was a sign that within two minutes I would be asleep.

Sitting up I fought slumber, wanting to enjoy the room I had thought of throughout my day touring Thimphu's holy sites.

The next thing I knew sunlight streamed onto my bed and a loud knock played at my door.

It was time to start a new day.

Chapter Twenty-Three

Thailand

A First Arrival to a Second Home

Bangkok
Thailand
2002

Of all my second homes around the world Bangkok comes first. This *City of Angles* that welcomes me, inspires me, and somehow calms and invigorates me in equal measure each and every stay.

Leaving my life behind in the UK I arrived in Bangkok's Don Muang airport. On landing I watched golfers wait on the side of the runway for our plane to pass before continuing their game.

Stepping from air conditioning's chill into a Thai afternoon's thick heat, I knew I was where I was supposed to be. I don't know how. I just did.

"Taxi," a voice shouted.

I looked to the beaten up white Fiat and nodded at its driver.

With a near toothless grin he left his car and rushed to me. Taking my backpack he threw it onto the taxi's backseat and ran back to his.

"Quick," he shouted, looking back to the line of new shiny official taxis he had just pushed in front of.

The taxi driver laughed again as I jumped into his moving car.

Paying a little extra we drove on Bangkok's super highway, an overhead bypass allowing those willing to pay to arrive in Bangkok's centre a half hour earlier than a usual two.

My driver talked to me in Thai. I couldn't understand a word. It was my first visit to Thailand. It was my first visit to Asia.

I still carried some tan from three months earlier when in the South Pacific islands of Fiji and The Cook Islands. Those paradises seemed as far away now as an England just left.

For a slight moment a hint of panic arrived to me. I had sold everything. I no longer owned a house, as did I no longer own the barber shop which had provided me with an income. I was homeless with just a backpack and a bank account to my name. Fantastic. This was the only word I could muster sitting in that taxi. In that moment any panic left me - not once has it reappeared since.

The taxi driver continued to speak to me in his own language. I had no idea the country I had only just arrived in would become home for the next three years. Nor did I know the words spoken to me now would become clearer as the years went by. In less than two years I would be able to hold a conversation with other taxi drivers delivering me to and from Bangkok airport's arrival and departure gates.

My taxi driver reached for a small glass bottle at his side. He took a swig and handed it to me to try. The high energy drink was different to the concoction I knew. It had the consistency of syrup.

Declining his offer I looked to my feet. I jumped as a large brown cockroach scurried across my toes.

The taxi driver gave another near toothless grin. With one hand on the steering wheel he leant down towards my feet. I closed my eyes as he hunted, not wanting to see the road ahead the taxi driver paid no attention towards.

With a laugh he sat up and returned his view to Bangkok's busy super highway. Holding his hand up he laughed again. The offending cockroach wriggled between a dirty finger and thumb.

The taxi driver's joy continued as he dissected the cockroach with a long grubby thumbnail.

Throwing the insect's still wriggling two halves out of his window, he took another draft of his syrupy concoction and accelerated.

The word fantastic came to mind once more. Looking to Bangkok's nearing skyline this was when my life truly began.

With a hotel found and an afternoon sleep made I walked out into my first Bangkok evening. Khao San Road was my destination.

Following a neon light haze hovering above a backpacker's sought after destination, I at last stood at the bottom end of Khao San Road.

At just 1,345 feet/410 metres long and once home to Bangkok's rice markets, Khao San Road is lined with shops and stalls selling handicrafts, clothes, books and a wide range fake of CD's and IDs. The bars and restaurants squeezed between these shops come to life after dark. As music booms out from bars filled with tourists, hawkers pass by carrying trays selling everything from wooden elephant ornaments to barbecued scorpions and spiders.

In 2002, Khao San Road had an edge to it. It was a place where anything could happen, good or bad. A time when elephants walked the streets – a painted trunk reaching out to foreign visitors for Thai Bhat notes, the beast's owner keen for any cash rewards given.

I watched Khao San Road change over the following two decades. Those roaming elephants disappeared, as did Khao San's once gritty road and pavement – replaced by neat tile and smooth road, making Bangkok's travellers haven more accessible for families.

Although Khao San Road still remains as special as ever, part of me misses those early days of excitement and danger once had. An edge far removed from today's more sedate setting.

After walking up and down that street on that first night, I found a bar about halfway up Khao San. There I found a friend, one who I would travel with in an eventual group of four to Phuket, Cambodia and back to Bangkok again.

This was my first day and night in Bangkok. Moments of awe and wonder, and of friendships made.

Over the next two decades Bangkok would be part of my life.

At the top of Khao San Road stands a white walled Buddhist temple - the centuries-old Wat Chana Songkhram. This became the temple I would visit each time on returning to the Thai capital. As I learnt to meditate under the instruction of a Northern Thai monk, I would sit crossed legged on Wat Chana Songkhram's bright red carpet, eyes closed within the temple's cool respite.

Around those temple walls and leading to the Chao Phraya River, the cul-de-sac of Bang Lamphu is lined with budget hotels, restaurants and coffee shops. This is home for me when in Bangkok.

Living in Chiang Mai I would ride my scooter down to Chiang Mai Airport, chain it up and buy a flight to Bangkok – this one hour flight cost just $15 then. With a day shopping in the capital and a night of dancing, drinking and laughter, a cheap hotel was found.

With a return flight back to Chiang Mai the next day, I would jump on my awaiting scooter and ride back to my apartment.

A return to Bangkok in 2009 saw me arrive at the beginning of political demonstrations against the government. A military crackdown followed as 100,000 people demonstrated in central Bangkok.

So too would I arrive in Bangkok as a coup d'état began, when in the May of 2014, Bangkok's streets where filled with soldiers and tanks, with a curfew set in place as the Thai military established a junta (National Council for Peace and Order) to govern the nation.

All these moments added to my love for the city. A city open twenty-four hours a day, seven days a week. A capital of smiles, of street food, of tuk-tuk rides and much preferred taxi bikes.

There were always three things I would do when arriving back to Bangkok after months away in Nepal, India or Cambodia. The first would be to visit Wat Chana Songkram, then in the evening I would take a taxi bike east across the city to the cinema in MBK's vast shopping mall. I would complete my three wants by watching a latest movie there. Those taxi bike riders came to know me by name – and my destination.

In 2019 a return to Bangkok saw me staying in a rooftop hotel suite. It was a room stayed in many times before for over a decade.

One night while watching neon lit boats pass by on the Chao Phraya River, I turned and looked across that rooftop.

It was filled with memories of other times, and of those who had once accompanied me there.

Chapter Twenty-Four

Nepal

Earthquakes, Stupas and a Sauna

Kathmandu
Nepal
April 2016

In the April of 2016, Nepal's first high season of the year was coming to a close. Hosting more tourists than the country's previous autumn months, the thought of returning tourism eased Nepalese minds. This gave hope to a future when Kathmandu's tourist area of Thamel would be alive with visitors again.

Those spring visitors made back to their own countries as the 2015 earthquakes' one year anniversary approached.

Work came in the form of documenting a handful of villages damaged by both 2015 earthquakes. It would mean a three hour drive north east of Kathmandu. This was a route I knew well.

Following Sir Edmund Hillary's footsteps once more along a well-known road, our diplomatic jeep was followed by one of the United Nations' fleet - the letters UN displayed on its rooftop and sides in a familiar blue.

I was to photograph a working conjunction of the Finnish embassy, The United Nations and the World Wildlife Foundation.

My job was to document the results of disaster relief provided by all parties over the previous year. This would involve a three day trip leaving Kathmandu Valley and venturing into Nepal's northern jungle forests.

Setting off in early morning to beat the capital's notorious rush hour traffic, we bypassed the ancient city of Bhaktapur as dawn faded. We travelled north until arriving at Sindhupalchowk, one of Nepal's seventy-seven districts. A narrow trail led us to our first village. Soon becoming a dust laden track of potholes and bumps each driven mile was felt.

Within thirty minutes we reached our destination, a barren landscape coated in parched rust coloured soil. A mixture of new and damaged homes completed the setting. The scene gave the appearance that the previous year's earthquakes had only just happened an hour before our arrival.

This was how it was with the majority of other villages visited. Within every community there was a combination of homes either repaired, newly built or untouched. The effects of 2015's earthquakes were apparent in a variety of ways, from deep cracks running from rooftop to ground across aged stone walls, to homes which no longer had rooftops.

Walking round this village settlement it was clear little had been achieved over the following year since the earthquake. Some water tanks and sanitary blocks had been constructed by the organisations I photographed for now, yet these were seldom used by those they had been provided for. The villagers had resorted back to using centuries old traditions to aid their daily lives.

Water was still obtained by filling a bucket lowered down by a weathered rope into what seemed a bottomless well, and a natural underground stream's seep into the village centre was adequate for laundry and bathing; much the way it had been for hundreds of years.

In the background of planned plots for more sanitary blocks young families had begun to repair their homes themselves. The promised US$2,000 the government had allocated to every home that had applied for funding had yet to be seen.

In order to qualify for funding all applicants were to observe building regulations. To be paid in three instalments, many people in rural areas found difficulty accessing these funds as they did not have bank accounts.

By the time of the earthquake's first anniversary the first payment of funding had only been made to seven hundred households countrywide. It would not be until after the disaster's second anniversary that those monies would begin to trickle towards households in need.

There was a problem with the rebuilding undertaken by those no longer willing to wait for their government. Mortar or concrete was unavailable to hold reclaimed bricks in place. In the tradition of their ancestors a mixture of water, clay, tall grass leaves and soil was used. This only confirmed why Nepal's villages had seen to so many fatalities. This traditional way of building proved inadequate to resist the force of a seven or more magnitude earthquake.

Two more villages were visited over the following days. Each one had the same problems as the others. All communities awaited their promised funds, they also took to repairing their homes themselves using the same weak mortar as was tradition.

Our journey back to Kathmandu after three days was diverted due to a landslide. A common occurrence for the time of year, when fine talcum powder dust plays beneath steep hillside rock beds.

An alternative route taken was extremely rough along our rutted hillside track. It wasn't until arriving in Kathmandu later that night that we discovered we had driven above a 5.6 magnitude aftershock, its epicenter 6 miles/10 km directly beneath us.

Driving back into the capital and weaving through its maze of narrow roadways and lanes we arrived at guarded embassy gates. The diplomat beside me smiled.

"I rang ahead," she told me. "It's ready for us."

It wasn't until those embassy gates closed behind our jeep that I saw what she meant. What I suppose makes every Nordic embassy complete. There in the middle of the compound gardens sat a large wooden sauna fired up and awaiting our arrival.

The evening ran into the early hours accompanied by visits to the steaming sauna shipped in especially from European homelands, and cold beers beneath a Nepalese night sky filled with stars.

*

An official ceremony had been put in place to mark the first anniversary of Nepal's 2015 earthquake. This was to be held in Durbar Square as nightfall came.

Given access to a rooftop bar overlooking the event, those of us who had shared an evening of sauna and drinks watched the ceremony unfold as one hundred volunteers lit candles placed across Durbar's red brick floor. The outline of these memorial candles were arranged in the shape of the Kasthamandap Temple and Dharahara Tower, both of which had been destroyed in the disaster.

As the night sky darkened Durbar Square came to light. As shrine and tower flickered with amber licks 'We Will Rise' was spelt out above the scene by an equal amount of small prayer candles. Those candles which had burnt so brightly in reproduction of once cherished structures signified an end to past events. Now it was time for Nepal to move forward.

The evening drew to a close and the people of Kathmandu returned to their homes. Myself and the diplomat who had introduced me to my first ever sauna took a walk though one of Kathmandu's remaining earthquake induced homeless communities - those who still lived in tents of tarpaulin and sand bags on the edge of Kathmandu's Tibetan temple grounds of Boudhanath.

Boudhanath's white dome stupa topped by a golden spire is a main attraction for the capital's visitors. A constant flow of Tibetans and burgundy robed monks and nuns walk around the stupa in a clockwise direction, the all-seeing eyes of Buddha painted below a glistening spire watching everyone below who follows his path.

Under the shadow of Boudhanath Stupa the tented city had grown since its inception just days after April's 2015 earthquake. Those who had lost their homes were joined by those who feared sleeping inside theirs.

As the two of us walked through the site it was plain to see many had returned to their homes.

This was not what we had really come to see. Looking back I recognise how our conversations held a sense of debriefing, not so much for what we had experienced and seen over the previous three days, but for our own wellbeing when surrounded by everyday scenes of another's hardship and loss. It is a fondly remembered walk. A walk that with all its sorrowful connotations was accompanied by a lightness and jollity between us both.

Chapter Twenty-Five

Myanmar

Golden Pagodas, Lessons and Slums

Yangon
Myanmar
January 2015

One week earlier I had been in Mumbai, India. It had been my birthday.

On that birthday night I flew direct from Mumbai to Bangkok.

Back in my second home, I spent the next five days in my usual rounds of cinema, coffee shops and shopping. These activities were made in early morning or evening. Most daylight hours were spent in an air conditioned hotel room, either writing or processing photographs on the small laptop which fit snug into my camera bag.

On my sixth day back in Bangkok I flew to Yangon, Myanmar – once known as Rangoon, capital of Burma.

It wasn't until standing in line at Yangon Airport's immigration counter that I recalled moments encountered ten years earlier. My one unofficial visit to the country I now tried to enter.

The thousand yard stares of child soldiers came to mind, and the Keren National Liberation Army grounds I had once documented.

Worry to my being in Myanmar faded. That was until a chance conversation with a westerner with many years' experience living in Myanmar.

"Have you seen the list in your hotel?" She asked me.

The mention of a list brought back some anxiety experienced at Yangon's immigration. I told her no. Then she explained.

"Every night at 6pm, hotels call the government and read off a list of westerners staying in their rooms that night."

This meant a tourist's whereabouts for their whole trip could be followed by those in power. Telling her of my last journey to Myanmar, I asked if I was on a different kind of list.

"Most probably," she said matter-of-factly. "They'll defiantly be aware you're in their country."

I flew back to Bangkok a couple of days later.

Even though refusing to publish the photos of those child soldiers a decade ago they had eventually been published in the world press. My Myanmar excursion was cut short by moments captured in the past.

Recalling those liberation army photos on my flight back to Bangkok, I wondered if any of those young soldiers pictured had made it into maturity.

Chapter Twenty-Six

Morocco

Carpets, Souks and Captains

Tangier
Morocco
1997

Morocco's northern city of Tangier became clearer with each advance made. From the ferry's top deck, I watched flying fish skim over white crescent waves burning bright in midday sun, the Spanish port of Algeciras fading in the distance behind me with every passing second.

Flying from England to Malaga, I took a bus ride south along Spain's eastern coastline to the town of Algeciras. From there I boarded a ferry to Morocco's north-western tip and the harbour town of Tangier, a strategic gateway between Africa and Europe since the Phoenician times of 1500 BC.

The ferry docked into Tangier with a bump. With my backpack across one shoulder I followed the other passengers then stepped onto Tangier's docks. I saw what I was looking for straight away.

Walking to the ticket office I bought a one way ticket to Casablanca. My bus was leaving in one hour.

A local approached me with a broad smile.

Partaking in usual banter of where I was from, going to, and for how long, he asked if I would like to see his brother's carpet shop.

"I'm not buying anything," I told him. "I can't carry a carpet round with me anyway," I added.

Telling me he understood and that all I have to do is look, he grinned as I nodded ok.

"I've only got an hour," I said, as he led me through market places akin to tales of lamps and genies. We came to a stop outside a one shop. A heavy curtain covered its doorway.

"Here," the man said. Pulling the curtain aside he ushered me in. The shop fell dark as its heavy curtain fell back into place behind me.

"This way," my guide said. He led me down some stone stairs and into a cellar lit with several long florescent tube lights. To my relief the place was filled with carpets, not an imagined lone chair, today's newspaper, cable ties and a hood.

"I'm not buying anything," I said again.

"I know, I know. Just look."

The man's *brother* joined us and together they began to show me huge detailed carpets.

"They're too big," I told them. They immediately brought some smaller carpets out – one by two metres in size.

"We know you don't want one," the guide said. "But, if you did. Which one would you have?"

"That one," I said and pointed to the small carpet of white with neatly stitched blue, red and green shapes across it. The carpet was rolled up, put into a bag and handed to me before I could say no.

"I don't want it," I said. "I told you I wasn't going to buy anything. I don't want it."

I felt the chill of the wall behind me as the large hand on my chest pushed me back.

"I don't want it, I don't want it," my guide said inches from my nose. "What are you, a baby?"

"Alright," my young ego took hold. "I'll have it."

After ten minutes haggling I made it back to Tangier's port, a heavy backpack digging into my shoulders and an unwanted carpet rolled up under one arm. Stowing my carpet in the harbour side locker room I had been told of, I put the pink ticket needed to retrieve my carpet in my wallet and caught a bus to Casablanca.

Casablanca wasn't like it was in the movies.

Any romantic ideas towards the city were banished by a grey cityscape of industrial chimneys, each one billowing out noxious fumes in what is known as the economic capital of Morocco.

My first night in Morocco was spent in a small hotel near Casablanca's Atlantic coastline. The next day my morning was spent walking through streets of Casablanca's French colonial legacy of Mauresque architecture - a blend of European art deco and Moorish design. After lunch I visited The Hassan II Mosque.

Watching over surfers playing amid the Atlantic's cold waves, The Hassan II Mosque welcomes up to 105,000 worshipers to gather for prayer at any one time. The 7th largest mosque in the world and costing 700 million USD, The Hassan II Mosque was built in the style of Moorish architecture under the guidance of King Hassan II. It was completed in 1993. Standing tall is a 690 feet/210 metre minaret. Sixty stories high and topped by a laser, its beam is directed towards Mecca.

After an afternoon walking beneath The Hassan II Mosque's huge retractable roof and exploring rooms with walls of hand-crafted marble it was time to leave Casablanca. I headed southwards once more. A three hour bus ride later I arrived in Marrakech, a world away from Casablanca's tranquil mosque and its polished marble floors.

Finding a hotel I then walked to Marrakech's famous Jemaa el-Fna square. I arrived as dusk began.

To the sound of mosques calling devotees to prayer, I watched a purple sky turn to night above the chaos of Jemaa el-Fna.

Located in Marrakesh's Medina quarter, the square of Jemaa el-Fna is a market place by night offering its visitors orange juice stalls, leather goods, all manner of fruit, and all types of meat obtained from all types of animals. Smoky wisps of barbequed dishes hover above the square enticing all below.

By day Jemaa el-Fna is filled with snake charmers, magicians, merchants of traditional medicines, and story tellers sit encircled by those listening to tales spoken in Berber or Arabic. Once I saw a man sitting before a small table filled high with popcorn. Looking closer it wasn't popcorn. The table was stacked with teeth. Each molar or incisor waiting patiently for its new owner.

Along one side of the square is Marrakesh's souk. This traditional

North African market provides the daily needs of the locals in the way of food, household goods and clothing.

Behind the square runs a maze of alleyways and narrow streets. This tangle of lanes often opens up to reveal leather makers using techniques handed down for generations.

I would walk through these ancient habitats for hours over the following two days. When I thought I knew where I was a corner would be rounded that would throw me off track once more. Finding my way from that Moroccan labyrinth I would take coffee at the Café Argana, where the best view of Jemaa el-Fna's delights can be found.

With a return flight from Malaga to the UK pulling on me, I left Marrakech for Tangier. This I did by night train. My sleeper car had six bunks, three on either side of an impossibly small carriage. Mine was a top bunk. It was hard to sleep on your back with the ceiling two inches from your nose.

Travelling north through the night to Tangier, if I timed it right I could pick up my carpet and catch the next ferry to Algeciras. From there a bus journey to Malaga would see me boarding my plane homewards. Simple. Or so I thought.

Arriving in Tangier I rushed to the locker room with a now tattered pink ticket. The locker room was locked. Peering through a dusty window I saw the man who had locked my carpet away days earlier. He was asleep.

Looking to my pink ticket and then to my return ferry ticket I wondered what to do. My ferry was leaving in twenty minutes. I was determined not to go without my carpet. I hammered on the metal shutter before me. I didn't stop until a groggy locker room man opened up with a frown. My carpet returned to me, I ran to the ferry. I was stopped at its gangway before I could board.

"The captain wants a word with you," I was told.

The ferry captain walked down the gangway and stared at me. He then began to tell me off for being late. I was going to tell him about the rolled up carpet under my arm I was too tired to.

"Look," I said. "Are you going to let me on or not?

The captain said nothing and walked up his ferry's wooden gangway. I followed. Once we had set sail I watched Tangier slowly fade from sight.

And what happened to the carpet? I still have it. It has been at the foot of my bed in every home I have ever had – in the UK that is.

Chapter Twenty-Seven

INDIA

Taxis, Kites and Ghats

Varanasi
India
December 2014

Crossing over the Nepal/India border, my friend and I stepped onto Indian soil together.

Our bus to Varanasi arrived. Its black curtained windows didn't look inviting. A taxi driver called out to us.

It may seem an extravagance to take a four hour ride by taxi, but split between two it didn't cost much more than a promised six hour journey by bus. So a taxi it was.

There is one thing which always amazes me when crossing over from one country into another. Every time it's the same. Within feet of leaving one country it is obvious you are in a different land. This is not only due to the people. Buildings and countryside change within moments and there is a definite altered feel about the place.

Leaving Nepal behind those differing landscapes happened in an instant. From our taxi window there was not a sign of southern

Nepal's lush green jungle forests or mist laden marshes. Only endless fields of brown grasslands fell into view.

Arriving in Varanasi the city's Old Town provided our hotel. It was then that I realised Varanasi's significance within Indian culture and tradition.

Varanasi is seen as the spiritual capital of India. Dating from the 11th century BC, it is recognised as the oldest city in the world which still exists today.

Every year millions of Hindu pilgrims visit Varanasi's riverfront steps leading down to the banks of the River Ganges. These ancient steps are known as Ghats. Many pilgrims endure long journeys to visit these Ghats and take a holy dip in the Ganges - to wash away their sins in this lifetime, the last and those to come.

With a total of eighty-eight Ghats running parallel with Varanasi's Old Town most are for bathing and puja (prayer) ceremonies. Two Ghats are used exclusively to perform funeral rites and are seen as cremation sites. This is what I had come to photograph. Another culture so diverse to my own - in a city with close to two thousand temples and shrines located on its winding streets.

That first evening saw us sitting at our five story hotel's terraced rooftop. Dusk's beginnings signalled the flight of hundreds of kites.

High above kites danced and swooped left to right from pulling hands on surrounding rooftops. Each kite battled its neighbour with razor sharp twine aimed to cut another kite's thread. Dozens of kites fell over Varanasi's Old Town that evening, all to a backdrop of purple and red Indian skies.

The next morning we took a boat trip along the sacred waters of the River Ganges.

From my vantage point fifty feet from the Ghats, I took photos of those washing, praying, swimming and doing their laundry in green holy water - capturing a pilgrim's devotion held within religious rites.

Leaving those in prayer behind we sailed to the last of the Ghats, Manikarnika Ghat.

Around one hundred bodies a day are cremated on wooden pyres along Manikarnika's riverbanks. The largest and most auspicious of Varanasi's cremation Ghats, it operates twenty-four hours a day, every day of the year.

Our boatman told us photographs were not allowed. I took two shots. The boatman immediately swung our boat around in haste.

My first shot was a macabre scene of eighty or so people lining the riverbanks of Manikarnika's funeral Ghat. All watched their loved one's remains being released into the River Ganges.

My second photograph was of those same people. Only now each one stood with an arm outstretched as eighty fingers pointed at my camera lens.

For what was to happen the following day I should have taken those pointing fingers as a sign - as well as heeding a boatman's words when told photographs were not permitted.

The next day we had become a group, as is often the way when travelling. The two of us were joined by a Greek girl, her Brazilian boyfriend and a German woman. The five of us set out together to walk the length of the Ghats.

Seeing funerals taking place on smaller Ghats confirmed lessons of impermanence encountered in my studies of Buddhism. The same was true in Hindu beliefs - the physical form is merely a vehicle of the soul.

Watching those bodies alight brought a disassociation towards what you were seeing. This only highlighted understandings that the bodies now aflame were not those who had once lived a life, had breathed, walked, laughed, cried, and acted out all manner of emotions akin to the human condition. The bodies slowly being reduced to cinders before me were only a shell of what had once housed a loved one's spirit.

Moving along those settings of prayer and last rites we arrived at our final Ghat, Manikarnika Ghat. The Ghat I had taken forbidden photos of from a boat the day before. This time I decided to be a little more subtle.

Setting my camera to a good shutter speed and aperture, I positioned my jumper over my camera so only the lens poked out.

Entering Manikarnika Ghat was similar to crossing over into another country. All changed within a few footsteps.

Up to five funeral pyres burnt steadily beneath a darkened sky of soot and ash. Mourners tended to an alight loved one's final passage from piles of wood beside them.

Cows ate from piles of hay beside smouldering ashes, and laundry dried beside the heat generated from burning bodies. With this spectacle before me I started to take my photos.

After taking ten frames I felt a hand wrap around my arm.

"No photographs," the man told me.

"I haven't got a camera," I said, my thumb quickly rewinding my cameras display dial.

The man pulled my jumper away to reveal my camera.

"Oh," I smiled, trying to use a little humour.

On my camera's display I showed him photos taken a week earlier of the monks in Lumbini, Nepal, the birth place of Buddha. This was how far I had rewound my photos back.

"No, you have rewound them," he said. Then he showed me his police badge. "You are coming with me to the police station."

My reaction was as always in these situations. I froze.

The shouting began.

The Brazilian of our party had seen what had happened. He rushed to my side. With all his Latino blood he exploded. Waving his hands and talking at great speed he told the undercover policeman I was not being taken anywhere.

I must admit I was quite envious of his outburst. Even though I do have my moments, I could never dream of achieving such an outpouring of focused emotion, not with my imbedded English reserve at least.

It worked. The policeman let me go.

Regaining my composure we left Manikarnika Ghat. I was more than thankful for an appearance of Latino fury.

Returning back to the hotel terrace and running my fingers through my hair it felt thick with dust. Rubbing my hand vigorously across my scalp triggered a flurry of ash to escape onto the floor.

I then reached for my trainer to release the small stone I had felt beneath my foot for most of the afternoon. It wasn't a stone, it was a souvenir from Manikarnika Ghat.

Chapter Twenty-Eight

Japan

A Visit to Kyoto and Hiroshima

Kyoto
Japan
December 2016

Travelling from Tokyo to Kyoto took two and a quarter hours to cover a distance of 282 miles/454km. This wasn't surprising considering a bullet train reaches speeds of 224mph/360kmph.

On arrival into Kyoto's main train station it was clear Japan's former capital until 1869 was very different to a bustling Tokyo.

Overlooked by the Hiro Mountain Range bordering on the Yamashiro Basin, Kyoto entertains Japan's cultural heritage. Classical Buddhist temples and Shinto shrines stand on what seems every street corner and Kyoto's size and layout makes the city easy to walk around.

A stroll beside traditional wooden houses along the banks of the Kamo River leads to Kyoto's Gion district in the east of the city. This was one of two reasons for my journey to the city - to photograph the Okiyas (tea houses) frequented by the maikos and geikos trained in the subtle art of the geisha.

There were geishas everywhere. Or so I thought. Those who walked Gion District's Hanami-koji Street were visitors the same as I. The only difference was that I hadn't hired a traditional kimono to wear for the occasion, neither was I in full makeup.

Although no true geishas were to be seen, the views of those dressed in flower pattern kimono of varying colours made up for this. They too walked the same cobbled stone street as geishas of a bygone age. Hanami-koji Street was alive with Japan's traditional outfit. An outfit which is as popular today as when first introduced centuries ago.

A figure walked towards me on the opposite side of the street. Dressed in a white kimono covered with deep red embroidered flowers I took one shot as she passed by.

It wasn't until I uploaded the day's photographs that I saw the woman's white profile with closed eyes. With a black background merging with jet black hair, a stray strand reached down across brow, cheekbone and slight jawline. A portrait of pensive thought captured in a moment.

My second reason for travelling to Kyoto was found to the west of the city. The bamboo forests of Arashiyama.

Overlooking Togetsukyo Bridge and the waters of the Ōi River, Arashiyama has been a popular destination since first discovered by nobles of Japan's hierarchy in the Heian Period of 794 to 1185.

Against a backdrop of lush green stems and tranquil grounds of the Fushimi-Inari-Taisha Shrine and Kinkaku-ji Temple, a red torii gate marks the entrance to Arashiyama's bamboo forest - a network of walkways overshadowed by the gentle sway of thick, towering bamboo trunks.

It was my last day in Kyoto. Saving the bamboo forests for last I planned to arrive in late afternoon when the light would prove best.

I took the local bus for my one hour journey to the bamboo forests I had come to see. The scenery travelled through began to look the same. An hour after boarding I arrived back outside my hotel. I had got on the wrong bus and taken a loop of the city.

It didn't bother me that I had been on a little tour of downtown Kyoto. I quite enjoyed being on the bus and watching the world go by. What did bother me was the day's dimming light.

If I was to photograph these bamboo forests I only had one chance to take the right bus second time around.

Another one hour bus journey later I arrived at Arashiyama's red torii gate entrance. I still had the light to contend with.

Racing beneath arching bamboo stems I at last found the scene I wanted.

The reduction of light I had worried about throughout my journey was of little consequence. The last of the day's Asian sun still held its strength, albeit in fine ochre shards breaking through green bamboo towers on either side of me.

An added result of my taking the wrong bus was that tourists of the day had left before the onset of dusk. This sparseness provided photographs capturing the solitude of the forest. The creak of bamboo was my only company.

With photographs taken of Kyoto's natural beauty it was time to board another bullet train.

This time it would be a one and a half hour journey at speed covering the 219 miles/354km from Kyoto, and through the cities of Osaka and Okayama to reach Hiroshima.

Hiroshima
Japan
December 2016

The largest city on Japan's biggest island of Honshu, Hiroshima's population of over one million lives on the coastline of the Seto Inland Sea. Along the banks of the Ōta River six channels divide the city into several islands. These isles are connected by the Hirode trolley car system.

My first destination was the location of what mind falls to on hearing the city's name. The Genbaku Dome, the only remaining building left standing at the hypocentre of an atomic blast.

At 8:15am on the 6th August 1945, United States airmen dropped the atomic bomb *Little Boy* onto Hiroshima from the American B-29 bomber The Enola Gay.

Detonating approximately 2,000 feet above the city, *Little Boy* killed 70,000 citizens instantly. By the end of the year injuries and radiation brought the total number of deaths to more than double this initial figure.

Genbaku's skeletal dome sits atop cracked walls and vast gaping holes where windows once sat.

The setting imposes a chilling reminder of past atrocities. I wonder what those US airmen would think today if they could see tourists from around the world taking selfies with their handiwork in the background.

A ferry ride from Hiroshima Bay took me to Itsukushima Island. Also known as Miyajima, the small island is revered for its forests and ancient temples. Miyajima is over run by more than a thousand Sika deer, considered in Shinto religion to be messengers of the gods.

Welcoming all visitors to Miyajima and marking the entrance to Itsukushima Shrine, the island's Floating Torii Gate stands just off shore in lapping waves. Made from deep orange camphor and cedar wood, the base of the torii gate's 55 feet/17 metre stance gives the impression it is balancing on the sea's surface.

My journey to Japan came together when finding the city's walled garden of Shukkei-en.

Set within the centre of Hiroshima's downtown area, this Edo Period landscape is set around a large pond fed by the waters of the Ōta River. The pond includes several islets which are spanned by traditional Japanese bridges.

Accompanied only by koi gliding gracefully through the water beside me, I found my stillness again.

All the distressing sights of earthquakes, volcanoes, slums and refugee camps left me, as did events of a distant past, where child soldiers hugged treasured rifles to them, and a country's people fought in the streets for democracy.

The life I had led over the previous decade and a half was cleansed, exorcised by the beauty unveiled in the simplicity of a Japanese garden.

Now those chapters were closed.

Chapter Twenty-Nine

Sri Lanka

Cricket, Riots, Buddha and Buses

Colombo
Sri Lanka
2012

I finally arrived in Colombo.

As the last plane to leave a snowbound Manchester Airport, a late departure meant a twenty-four hour stay in Dubai (hotel provided). Now I was at my destination, one day short of a ten day stay.

It was hot. In Colombo airport I found a bathroom and changed from English winter clothes into shorts and t-shirt – performing a balancing act in a small cubical in the process.

It was good to be back in tropical heat again. Those first days of Thai heat encountered all those years ago have never left me. Life's too short to be cold

A taxi delivered me to Colombo's train station. Planning to visit the cave system of Dambulla and its collection of ancient Buddha statues I would first need a train to the town of Kegalle, a three hour train ride north of the capital.

There were only third class tickets left.

Buying my ticket for the price of a cup of coffee back home, I walked the platform until finding my carriage. Colombo's train station manager ran up to me.

Showing him my ticket he shook his head.

"You are English?" He asked.

"Yes," I answered. He took his hand in mine and began to smile.

"I have to thank you," he said.

"For what?"

"For cricket."

This was the first time I had come across this. In years to come I would meet with the same thanks across India and Nepal for my country inventing cricket.

"You're welcome," I told him. Not being a cricket fan I couldn't think what else to say.

He took my ticket from me and led me further up the platform. On seeing first class was full he led me back.

"Here, sir," he ushered me into the train's second class carriage. "We can't have a countryman of cricket's birthplace in third class."

Thanking him again I found a seat. For the next three hours I battled sleep until arriving in Kegalle.

Not especially a tourist destination I somehow found a place to stay for the night. A spacious room and a first encounter with a mosquito net. The next morning I took a local bus east across the country to Dambulla.

Local buses are the same across the world. On many occasions in China, Nepal and India, I have watched goats and chickens bleat and cluck above passengers in overhead luggage compartments. Sri Lanka proved no different.

This is what I enjoyed most about travelling. The rawness of life. Everyday living in parts of the world so unlike the one in which I was raised. The local bus from Kegalle to Dambulla took an hour and a half to cover 56 miles/90km. Its price? Half a cup of coffee back home. Now I was in the centre of Sri Lanka

Finding a place to stay in an old colonial style hotel with polished wood floors and well-kept gardens, I walked to the huge golden Buddha statue above the entrance of Dambulla's cave temple, also known as The Golden Temple.

Carved into the base of 525 foot/160 metre high Dambulla rock, The Golden Temple is composed of five caves - Temple of the Lord of the Gods, Temple of the Great Kings, Great New Temple, Western Temple and Second New Temple.

All five caves have a collection of over one hundred and fifty statues and paintings showing the life of Buddha. There are also paintings on the walls depicting Buddha's life in Nepal and India, from his conflict with temptation under the Bodhi Tree of Bodh Gaya, to Buddha's first sermon in Sarnath. These murals cover 23,000^{sq} feet/2,136^{sq} metres of Dambulla's cave walls.

Leaving Dambulla's caves I looked up to the huge golden Buddha statue which had seen to my arrival. I took one photo. That photo was an indication of the life I was to lead in two years' time, as it was featured in the UK's Daily Telegraph newspaper one month later.

I left one Buddhist setting for another. Taking another local bus for the same cost of another half cup of coffee, I arrived in Sri Lanka's second largest city, Kandy.

My reason for being in Kandy was to visit Sri Dalada Maligawa, also known as The Temple of the Sacred Tooth Relic.

Finding a hotel opposite the entrance to Kandy's Royal Palace complex, I waited until the next afternoon to see the ancient relic of Buddha's tooth. Instead I decided to explore the city. I found a riot.

From what I could gather a group of Kandy's students had begun to demonstrate peacefully. The high presence of army and police surrounding all had sparked the riot I now watched.

Camera in hand I was in my element. Memories of capturing Myanmar's civil war and Bangkok's military coups returned to me.

Any excitement left me as I watched an army colonel direct one of his officers to see what I was doing. I pressed the shutter as he pointed at me with scorn. Backing into the crowds I was gone and returned to my hotel.

After an evening of looking around the city I woke the next morning ready to see Buddha's tooth.

Taken from Buddha's remains after his cremation in Kushinagar, India, it was smuggled into Sri Lanka and ended up in Kandy.

You can't actually see Buddha's tooth. It is hidden away in a series of seven gold caskets. Like a Russian Matryoshka doll, Buddha's tooth is kept within the smallest casket. Shaped like a stupa, these golden caskets are kept in a shrine inside Sri Dalada Maligawa temple.

Passing through a tunnel of painted murals I arrived at the first floor of The Temple of the Sacred Tooth Relic.

Following other visitors I stood before a velvet curtain. Behind that curtain sat a cushion with the seven gold caskets on top housing Buddha's tooth. A slight gap in the curtain allowed all to glimpse the tooth's caskets. This was enough for me.

With only a few days left in Sri Lanka I ventured south to Sri Lanka's beaches. The town of Habaraduwa was my destination.

It took two local buses and a tuk-tuk ride to reach Habaraduwa. With my journey split into two, it took six hours to travel the 137 miles/220km from Kandy to the city of Galle on the southwest coast of Sri Lanka. Both bus rides put together cost the equivalent of one English coffee. I had circumnavigated half of the country for the price of three coffees.

On each bus I found a backseat with an open window to look out of. The heat on those buses was stifling and I was glad to able to stick my head out of the window for most of my journey.

Arriving in Galle bus station I approached some backpackers. As I said hello one asked if I was ok. Replying yes and confused by their concern I found a tuk-tuk to take me the twenty minute journey to Habaraduwa. The tuk-tuk driver also looked at me with concern.

"Are you ok?" He asked.

"Yes," I said again, still unaware of the reason for other's concerns towards me.

I found a hotel and booked in. The receptionist handed me my key with a worried look.

"Are you ok?" She asked.

I just nodded with a smile and made for my room.

Putting my backpack down I walked to my hotel room's bathroom.

Turning on the light I looked at the mirror. Two green eyes and a set of teeth stared back. Moving forward I took a closer look. My face, neck and ears were covered in black soot.

I understood the concerns of backpackers, tuk-tuk drivers and hotel receptionists. As did I understand what happens when you have your head out of a bus window for six hours taking in traffic fumes.

Showered and changed, the hotel receptionist and I shared a smile on my way out to find some dinner, seeing I now understood her earlier concerns.

Chapter Thirty

Indonesia

A Squatter Slum Welcome

Jakarta,
Indonesia,
28th March 2015

Indonesia became another favoured place to stay. This new destination held the same sights and sounds as my other South East Asian haunts, making me feel at home in Indonesia's fast paced capital Jakarta.

Indonesia would become a place I would revisit often. Even if it was a destination to hold out in until flying back to Nepal - a feat I would have to carry out on occasion due to visa restrictions.

So too would I meet up with the friend I had travelled India with by taxis and night trains, their Dutch heritage more akin to Jakarta's architecture than mine - an enduring reminder of 16th century Dutch colonisation.

On another occasion I travelled from Jakarta, passing by Krakatoa and into northern Sumatra to document a volcano. Mount Sinabung on Sumatra's northeastern coastline had erupted only days after my arrival in Jakarta.

Flying to the volcano's nearest city of Medan, I made my way to document scenes of flowing lava and plumes of thick black ash rising high into the sky. It wasn't like that at all.

After a complicated five hour journey by rickshaw, taxi and two local buses, I was greeted by an ash white haze camouflaged in an equally white cloud sky. Mount Sinabung was nowhere to be seen.

I returned back to Jakarta and took an eight hour train ride into Java's central southern region to the city of Yogyakarta.

The only Indonesian royal city still ruled by a monarchy from its 18th century Sultan's Palace, Jogja, as it is known to locals, is a university city and seen as Indonesia's cultural centre for classical Javanese fine arts of batik, ballet, music, drama and literature.

As over ninety percent of Indonesia's 265 million citizens are of Muslim faith, I had a feeling my documenting of Buddhism had come to a pause. I was wrong. The world's largest Buddhist temple of Borobudur was just an hour's drive northwest of Jogja.

A construction of nine stacked platforms topped with a central dome, the 9th century Mahayana Buddhist temple is said to rival the temple complex of Cambodia's Angkor Wat.

Trips were organised to Borobudur at my guesthouse. I was promised a spectacular sunrise over sacred grounds, granted by a special pass allowing entry to the temple an hour before sunrise. Sunrise was to be at 4.30am. I didn't go. It was too early for me.

Instead I set about documenting Yogyakarta's street scenes.

Although pleased with my work in capturing the essence of this country new to me, I soon wanted to photograph something with a bit more of an edge to it. My want was granted one evening as dusk began.

It had rained that afternoon. Indonesia is one of the only countries in the world to have two monsoon seasons a year. Those afternoon downpours can flood a street within an hour only for its deluge to disappear as quickly as it arrived. Following each rainfall there would be a coolness in the air.

This respite to the day's searing humidity accompanied my walk towards the banks of Jogja's Code River.

From street level steep pathways led down to homes at the edge of the riverside. All had families sitting outside enjoying cool breezes from the flowing waters at their side.

Continuing onwards those houses at the bottom of sheer paths became less affluent. Continuing past a gap of wasteland a new pathway plummeted down into a collection of homes.

Families also sat out in the coolness of evening's start. There was one difference. There was a clear division between those of wealth and those of none. These were Jogja's riverside squatter slums.

Standing at the top of the slum's near vertical path a family below waved. They beckoned me to them.

Reeling off a couple of shots on my way I was greeted by smiles. As in many other similar situations encountered I was sure my invitation was to relieve a boredom within those invitees.

All said my welcome was good and raising my camera they were happy to have their photos taken. I was also welcome to walk around their collection of ramshackle homesteads.

Built from a collection of brick, corrugated iron sheets and blue plastic tarpaulin, these homes were no different to those met with in any other city's poorer communities.

With no access or funds to buy their own land many of Jogja's most deprived are forced to settle on government lands, to 'squat', an act which is becoming a housing solution for low-income urban populations throughout the developing world.

A waist high wall partitions these homes from a 20 foot drop into Code River's brown turbulent flow; currents greatly enhanced by the day's heavy rainfall.

Across the river were more slums. Each one a mirror image of the makeshift constructions around me.

I sensed the novelty of my presence wore off. It was time to leave. The smiles of those living in the slum remained, but I realised my time there had come to an end.

Ascending the near vertical path leading from the slums an elderly man followed my climb. His goodbye to me held the same inner happiness met with every time I ventured into realms of those living on the edge of society.

I told the guesthouse owner where I had been. He explained how over the last few years the Indonesian government had stepped in to help these squatter slums.

Well-funded community venture projects had resulted in improving housing quality by use of urban settlement schemes, improving facilities such as drainage, accessible stairs and garbage collections.

It seemed those in power chose to help their country's poorest. Aiding those with little. This was a common sight throughout Asian and South East Asian countries travelled.

With a week spent within the colonial architecture of the East Javen city of Malang, and a jeep trip to the 7,64 feet/2,329 metre active volcano of Mount Bromo, it was onwards to another one of Java's forty-five active volcanoes - Ijen volcano and its sulphur miners at work within its toxic fumes.

Chapter Thirty-One

Nepal

Maoists, Portraits and Refugees

Pokhara
Nepal
October 2014

I took a flight from Delhi to Kathmandu. The train I wanted to take me from India's capital to the border of southern Nepal was full. Either a flight or an arduous bus ride north was my only choice.

My flight proved fortuitous. The very same train I couldn't get a ticket for came off its tracks and crashed close to India's border with Nepal.

Landing into Katmandu it felt good to be back in Nepal. My first visit had been in 2004 with another visit in 2009. The Nepalese capital still held the same mystique of those earlier visits.

This would be where I would find a trip to Tibet. I was in no rush. I knew I was going. Having given my word to the Tibetan government in exile to take those important photos of illicit hotel constructions. I also carried a bundle of prohibited letters in my backpack, and don't forget the lipstick. My instincts told me it wasn't time to go.

As always I followed my intuition. I had learnt when out in the world that timing is everything.

So I stayed in Kathmandu. This is where I discovered portrait photography.

People, this has always been and still is my favourite subject. I can take or leave landscape, wildlife or event photography. Yes, I still enjoy capturing the scene and telling a story with documentary photography, but portraiture is my passion. Catching the soul of those before my lens.

Whenever in the field, be it taking photos for magazines or NGOs, when I know I have got my required shots then it is my turn to take portraits of those I have documented in their plight - portraiture learnt on the back streets of Kathmandu.

It took a while to build up confidence to approach a stranger and take their photo. Soon I developed a technique I still use to this day.

Finding my subject I walk up to them slowly. Holding eye contact, with a respectful smile I raise my camera slightly and smile again. If I see a glimmer of a yes their photo is taken in a second, so catching their true self straight away. Any longer and the portrait looks posed.

Most of the time people are happy to have their photo taken and see the results on my camera's display. There are those who refuse. I learnt the hard way not to continue with these. Not only are terse words directed your way, the resulting photo shows an unwilling subject. It carries something in their eyes. I suppose that something is they didn't want their photo taken.

Now I simply thank those who refuse and move onto the next. There is always someone who wants their photo taken. Kathmandu proved to be a mine of infinite portraits.

As the advent of dusk bathed the streets of Nepal with an amber glow I would walk from the tourist area of Thamel to Durbar Square, hunting for my quarry and taking portrait after portrait.

Looking at those portraits on my laptop years later, zooming in close you can often see my reflection in their eyes; holding my camera, frozen in time. Much the way those whose portrait has been taken are also.

After a few weeks in Kathmandu I was still not ready to go to Tibet. Instead I travelled six hours westwards by bus to the lakeside city of Pokhara.

I first visited Pokhara in 2004, staying by its tear shaped Phewa Lake for two and a half months. Pokhara was a different place then. Nepal was in the midst of civil war.

Beginning in 1996 and known as the Maoist Conflict, what followed would be a ten year armed conflict between the Communist Party of Nepal (The Maoists) and the government of Nepal.

The civil war was evident in 2004, not only for the distant sound of gunfire and mortar booms heard on occasion in surrounding forest hills, every evening at 6.30pm Nepal government troops would parade through the town. This was where I captured my first conflict photograph. A year before my time with Myanmar's liberation army.

Taken on film it shows the army readying themselves to march to show their prominence on the streets of Nepal's second largest city.

In the background of the photo an army sergeant can be seen looking into the lens and making his way towards me. I remember how he had towered above me demanding my roll of film. As he reached for my camera I held it behind my back and told him no. I had been taking photos all day. I wasn't going to give him or anyone else my precious thirty-six shots.

I showed him my British passport. I didn't know what that was supposed to do but it worked and he walked away.

It has always been beneficial to be British when travelling. Everyone speaks English and as a nation we are much liked in Asia and South East Asia. I like to think this is because we are polite, and have a good sense of humour.

It was good to be back beside that lake. It's still surface gave me a regained peace which heightened my new life on the road again, allowing me to settle completely into living out of a backpack, and be free to take photographs each day.

Every evening I would walk the small path beside those waters. I would stop at the lake's south-western edge where a small island stands a short boat ride away from the shore. From the Hindu shrine within the island's centre, a mist of incense smoke spreads its way inches above the lake's surface to the mainland.

Even though portraiture work was my prime focus I still photographed Phewa Lake, its fleet of bright blue and red painted boats adrift, Fishtail Mountain and the snowcapped peaks of the Himalaya's Annapurna Range in the distance.

From morning to early evening traders sat along Phewa Lake's path, a blanket spread out before them lined with bracelets, trinkets and small Buddha statues. Each waited for their wares to catch the eye of a passerby. These traders were all Tibetan. I had first encountered them beside the lake on my first arrival in 2004.

Stopping at one blanket of Tibetan trinkets its owner smiled.

"Are you going to buy something else?" She asked me.

A collection of wrinkles running in all directions across aged features were enhanced by her greeting.

I recognised her too, as it seems she did me.

"Yes," she said. "I remember you."

My smiles came too as I recalled my last day in Pokhara a decade ago. I had bought a ceremonial spoon with a dragon's head at the end of its handle from her. This was after promising I would buy something throughout my stay beside the lake.

Her recognition of me gave a feeling of home. Giving me the sense I was not so isolated whilst in these different lands. A subtle hint I belonged in this place so unlike the one in which I was born. A comfort held in the remembrances of another, if only for a moment.

Sitting with her I showed her a photo on my phone of the Dalai Lama taken only weeks earlier in McLeod Ganj. Taking the phone from me and raising it to her forehead His Holiness' portrait faced from her. A couple of her friends joined us. Each copied her actions before handing my phone back to me with a thank you.

I had witnessed these actions before when in McLeod Ganj. Only then it had been the Dalai Lama's printed photograph which was raised to the forehead of his devotees. I suppose it made no difference what medium his photo was on, the age of smart phones bringing a realisation of how times had changed since I last walked along Pokhara's waterfront.

Promising once more to buy something from her at the end of my visit, a promise upheld by another spoon, we talked a while longer. It was then I learnt of the Tashi Ling Tibetan Refugee Camp.

One of Pokhara's two Tibetan settlements, Tashi Ling was on the southern outskirts of the city.

"You must visit," the lady said, confirming what appeared to be another step on my path concerning Tibet.

I put off going to the camp for a couple of days, my intuition speaking again to wait a little while longer before going.

As always I followed my thoughts until arriving at Tashi Ling one sunny afternoon two days later.

Lines of prayer flags spread out from Tashi Ling's main building - five colours of blue, white, red, green and yellow representing the five elements of sky, air, fire, water and earth. Below those flags celebrations were at hand. At first I thought this was the camp's normal every day festivities. I soon learnt it wasn't.

Talking to a group of English people there I discovered I had arrived on Tashi Ling's 50th anniversary. On the very day of my arrival, half a century ago in the autumn of 1964, the Tashi Ling Tibetan Refugee Camp had become home to 399 Tibetans.

Fleeing Chinese oppression across the Tibetan Plateau and into Nepal's Mustang District, these refugees were found by three holidaying university students from England who then brought them to Pokhara. The result was the establishment of the Tashi Ling Tibetan Refugee Camp.

It was these former English students I talked with now. They had returned to Pokhara after five decades to celebrate Tashi Ling's Golden anniversary. Tashi Ling's community now has a thriving carpet weaving business and is home to over one hundred families.

To have arrived on that day seemed prophetic, not only for the course my journey took, but for my photography also.

One photograph taken that day confirmed my decision to go to Tibet and to take those photos for the Tibetan government - and to deliver the bundle of letters and cosmetics tucked safely away in my backpack.

A photographic display in Tashi Ling's main building depicted the journey from Mustang to Pokhara half a century ago, and the construction of Tashi Ling's refugee settlement.

A collection of aged faded photographs lined the walls. An elderly Tibetan lady pointed to a photo taken fifty years ago. The figure of a teenage girl smiled back from a bleak northern Nepalese landscape. That teenage girl was her. Taken on her journey to reach Pokhara's tranquil lakeside.

Capturing that moment made me all the more determined to carry out my plans in my nearing journey into Tibet.

Spending the rest of the afternoon taking portraits of those whose features resembled the one who had told me of this refugee camp, I felt a familiar stillness awaken within. I also felt humble. A sentiment produced in seeing those who had made a new life for themselves in another country through great adversity.

A week later after my visit to Tashi Ling I was back in Kathmandu.

Once more I sensed it was not my time to venture into Tibet. Instead I choose another destination. The Kingdom of Bhutan.

Chapter Thirty-Two

India

The Dalai Lama, Hotels and a Cake

New Delhi
India
4th January 2016

It wasn't so much a birthday party.

His Holiness the 14th Dalai Lama had become eighty years old on the 6th July 2015 the previous year. Now nearly six months later, His Holiness' closest friends through the years were to gather for a day of celebrations, congratulating him on reaching such an important milestone and to wish him a healthy and long life. I knew I had to go. Even if it meant chancing my luck.

The event was to be held in the Oberoi Hotel, a five star hotel located beside the foreign embassies within New Delhi. With my camera bag on my back I hailed a taxi. I arrived at the hotel gates twenty minutes later. They were closed.

Approaching the three policemen standing in front those gates I reached into my camera bag pocket. I took out my press passes.

I had three press passes. Two were from agencies I am signed with, one in Los Angeles the other in London. My third press pass was bought on Bangkok's Khao San Road for $10. With my photo and passport number across its front it looks more official than the other two. I showed the policemen all three.

With a nod they let me through the gates. Walking to Oberoi Hotel's entrance I was sure the Bangkok pass had got me in.

A second set of security stood at the hotel doors. This time there was an airport x-ray machine and metal detector. Showing all three passes again I was allowed entry and soon stood in the hotel lobby.

You could have been anywhere but India. Having been on the road for so long it had been a while since I had seen such opulence and finery. At the far end of the lobby was the doorway into the event I had come to photograph. Another x-ray machine stood there. As did four burly security guards.

Figuring I had made it into the hotel with relative ease I thought this wouldn't be a problem. It was.

Refused entry I tried again, and again. My instincts told me not to push the luck that had already seen me through two security points.

Deciding on a plan of action I returned to the lobby, remembering how comfortable the settees looked there. Finding one and settling back in comfort my second plan came to me. I would sit here until His Holiness arrived. At least then I might get some photos.

A man sat down beside me. Being around Tibetan people so often over the last year I recognised him as one.

"Tashi delek," I said to him.

He turned to me and repeated my hello in his own language.

"You have come to see His Holiness?"

"Yes, but they won't let me in."

The man glanced to the security who had refused me entry.

Asking why I was here I showed him my camera. Then it all came out. I told him of my journey to Tibet and the letters I had delivered back and forth to India. I left the bit about the lipstick out. I also told him of the photos I had taken for his government in exile.

He nodded as I talked. Excusing himself, he left me on the settee. Sure my chatter had caused his departure I settled back and continued my wait for the Dalai Lama's arrival. The man came back.

"Come with me," he said.

He led me past the security guards who had stopped me entering the hotel's main function room and handed me his business card. It read 'His Holiness the 14th Dalai Lama Security Officer'.

Around one hundred and fifty seats were set out before a small stage. On the right of the stage was a settee similar to the one I had enjoyed in the lobby. To the left a podium stood awaiting its speakers.

I was sent to the roped off press gallery at the back of the room. Once again I was the only westerner amongst several Indian photographers.

The seats were soon filled with people of all nationalities and creeds. A Jain high priest sat beside a Tibetan Rinpoche, their attire a stark contrast of white and burgundy robes, as was the Hindu priest dressed in orange taking his seat beside a white and blue swathed Brahmin of similar faith. Then His Holiness took to the stage.

I could tell the Dalai Lama was enjoying the same comfort on his settee as I had moments earlier in the lobby on mine, unaware I had been sitting next to one of his security officers.

The proceedings began with the tantric vocal chants of three Tibetan Buddhist monks. This unique form of throat singing is taught in the Gyuto Tantric Monastery in the foothills of the Himalayas close to McLeod Ganj, the place I had spent most of my time in India.

Little did I know that in two weeks' time I would be documenting those chanting monks of Gyuto standing before me, this time in their monastery home on the outskirts of Dharamsala as they prepared for their annual Puja ceremony.

The morning was filled with individuals sharing their stories of moments spent with the Dalai Lama. His Holiness listened intently to every word, nodding and sharing laughter with both speaker and audience in unison.

I caught His Holiness' smiles and expressions from the back of the room before a break was called for coffee and tea.

Filing out of the room there were tables of tea cups and chocolate cakes. Dignitaries and monks mingled together as I checked through photos captured that morning. Soon it was time to return to the celebrations.

The atmosphere in the function room had changed on my return. A serious demeanour was now replaced by a light heartedness, a settling into what was supposed to be a birthday party.

The security guards also seemed to be touched by the goodwill breezing through the room. I took my chance and dipped under the press gallery rope cordoning me off from the others.

Now it was His Holiness who took to the podium as I sat down in the aisle between his audience's seats.

As the Dalai Lama spoke I edged nearer and nearer to the stage until there was nowhere else to push forward to.

His Holiness had watched my advance and on reaching my limit he raised his hands in blessing to me. I caught the moment perfectly.

That was it. I knew I had got my photographs for the day. Now it was my time to enjoy the celebrations and listened to His Holiness' words to us all.

With the celebrations coming to an end the Dalai Lama stood and was helped down from the stage into the audience. Everyone left their seats and rushed to him.

Not liking crowds and seeing a mass of people begin to surround the Dalai Lama, I put my camera away, put my bag onto my back and left the function room. I stopped in the doorway and looked to the big piece of chocolate cake on the table to my right. It called to me.

I reached for it thinking I could eat it on the way back to my hotel in my own little celebration of the day. Before it was in my grasp a second crowd pushed forward into the function room taking me back in there with them.

I tried to leave again. I was stuck. My camera bag on my back was wedged between a pillar and a door. No matter how much I wriggled I couldn't break free. Then I looked to who walked towards me. It seemed His Holiness had seen my predicament. With a smile he took my hand in his and said a few words to me. Then he was gone.

Eventually managing to release myself from the door and pillar's grasp I watched His Holiness and his entourage leave.

Walking from the function room for a second time I looked to the big piece of chocolate cake from before. It was still there.

Walking from Oberoi Hotel's gates that evening I tried to rationalise the events that had just unfolded - my brief meeting with His Holiness the 14th Dalai Lama, brought about by the chocolate cake I now enjoyed on my walk homewards.

Chapter Thirty-Three

Thailand

Chiang Mai: Part I

Chiang Mai
Thailand
2002

Chiang Mai for me came in two time periods, each around eighteen months in duration. The following recounts my first stay.

Arriving in Chiang Mai in 2002 after three months exploring Bangkok, Koh Samui and Cambodia, an intended visit of ten days developed in to a near on year and a half stay.

After two month's living in a hostel in the western quarters of Chiang Mai's walled Old City, a house was rented between four. Our modern house stood behind our landlady's own traditional teak wood home. The landlady's sister kept an eye on us all. Especially me.

When getting back after a night out as dawn began to break, she would chase me up the path all the way to my doorstep - jumping as we went trying to clip me round the ear. She was only four feet tall.

One Christmas at the house a roommate showed with glee the Christmas Tree she had made.

"Where did you get the tree from?" I asked.

My roommate pointed to the garden between us and our landlady's house to where a chili tree once stood.

The chili tree belonged to the one who would always try to clip me round the ear for coming home too late. Most days I would watch her pick chili's for her lunch from the tree which now stood in our house adorned with tinsel.

The chili tree's owner walked in our house. Curious as to what Christmas was she tried to look at the tree behind us. Moving in the way of where she looked she eventually pushed me aside. On seeing her prized chili tree she ignored my roommate and jumped up and down trying to reach my head with an outstretched hand.

A scooter was rented and friends made. Nights were spent at the night market, or the cinema, or just sipping coffee watching the world go by.

Days were spent exploring the city by bike or by foot, with some voluntary work also, and taking regular runs up a winding hillside road to the temple Wat Doi Suthep, to work with the monk's communications for foreign visitors arriving to their sacred home.

It would be at the beginnings of early evening that the true wonder of Chiang Mai arrived for me.

With coffee and writing taking place at 5pm, a scooter ride back into the Old City across the moat surrounding it and through one of its four gates, I would arrive at the temple I had been shown in my first week in Chiang Mai.

The temple of Wat Chedi Luan would be a frequent part of my life throughout both chapters spent in Thailand's second largest city.

Each night at 6pm I would sit within Chedi Luan's temple upon worn red rugs splayed here and there over aged wooden floorboards, where small bird feathers lay having fallen from the rafters.

This was after a lighting of candles and three incense sticks, and placing a closed lotus flower in a vase beside rows of other candle and incense blessings.

Some evenings I would be alone but for an occasional Buddhist monk saying his prayers. Other nights I would sit beside a sea of orange robes and meditate as best I could, as were they.

A tall brick chedi (a Buddhist shrine with a large base topped with a spire) stood behind the temple. Built in the mid-15th century a modern day copy of an Emerald Buddha made from black jade was placed high in a reconstructed eastern niche.

Each night after time in the temple I would walk clockwise around the chedi a traditional three times - *in the magic hour* a friend had said as we walked together, a time when the light was perfect for photographs (a time which would come to good use in years to come). In fact a first foray into life as a documentary photographer began there.

Wat Chedi Luan was home to a lot of dogs, and I mean a lot.

Walking around the chedi in that magic hour it was not unusual for a visitor to get an occasional snarl directed at them. From the dogs that was, not the monks.

These temple dogs were allowed to roam free. Temple dogs in Thailand are also believed to be reincarnated monks who did not learn their prayers properly.

A local charity raised funds for these dogs so they may be fed and treated for the mange most carried, identified by the dry skin that covered the dogs' bodies, often more than fur. The charity noticed my regular visits to the temple and the camera I would often carry with me.

They asked me to take photographs of the dogs for publicity. This I did on merit and would often see my dog photos in coffee shops and restaurants around Chiang Mai, on posters and on the side of charity boxes placed on bar or counter.

Thailand's three day water festival of *Songkran* came and went, as did the lantern festival *Loi Krathong*, where I watched a quarter of a million candle lit paper lanterns float across the city I called home. Each lantern an orange dot following the thermals high above in lines and lines and lines.

Fireworks too came with the release of lanterns. Chiang Mai would become a haze of gunpowder smoke for days as a constant barrage of fireworks of all shapes and sizes would sound out. It was not a good time to be a westerner on a scooter. Foreigners were a prime target and I would often have to duck down as a firework whizzed over my head.

That scooter became such a large part of my life in Chiang Mai. From riding a winding mountainside road to the golden temple of Wat Doi Suthep to exploring an Old City's lanes and alleyways. At one time I could have drawn a detailed map within those old city walls.

At nights when sleep would not come, a scooter ride through empty streets would see a ride past the city's twenty-four hour flower markets - hitting a wall of rose scent mixed with Northern Thailand's 2am chilly hours.

Chiang Mai was a place where living was of ease and costs were low, giving chance to explore whatever you wanted to do or be.

The wanderlust that had directed me to Chiang Mai in the first place reared its head again.

After eighteen months of temples, friendships, scooters and early morning ear clippings, the call of the open road beckoned me to it again. I left Chiang Mai for Nepal.

Unbeknown to me then, I would return to Chiang Mai in under six months after a whirlwind trip from (wait for it): Nepal to the UK, to Canada to Mexico, Belize Guatemala, Honduras, Nicaragua, Costa Rica, then to America (Las Vegas, LA and Chicago), back to Canada, back to the UK, then to Seoul, South Korea for one month before returning to Thailand.

Arriving in Bangkok I flew to the island of Koh Samui on Thailand's east coast. I had no intention of returning to Chiang Mai.

Recuperating from all the travelling of the last six months I left for Koh Pang Yang after a few days - the island of full moon parties a thirty minute boat ride northeast of Koh Samui's eastern shoreline.

On my second day on Koh Pang Yang I received an email out of the blue one morning. An old friend was in Chiang Mai for the night. They asked if I was still lived in the city.

A boat ride back to Koh Samui, a flight to Bangkok and another flight saw me arrive back to Chiang Mai, just in time to spend an evening with the one who had enticed me back to my old home.

I would not leave Chiang Mai for another eighteen months.

Chapter Thirty-Four

Thailand

Chiang Mai: Part II

Chiang Mai
Thailand
2004

So, I found myself back in Chiang Mai again.

The friend I had travelled 900 miles/1,450km to see flew back to Singapore the next morning after my arrival.

All but two of those I had I known before in Chiang Mai where gone. Most had returned back to the *real* world, a want for a career and family overriding the ease and tranquility the city offered.

This was a reason why I had left for Nepal six months earlier also. Although life was good in Chiang Mai it proved too easy a life. I don't do easy. Yet, at this time I needed to stop travelling. I needed a home for a while. Chiang Mai seemed a good a place as any.

After a month in a guest house within the Old City I found an apartment with a spacious living room and bedroom, and a galley kitchen I only wandered into twice in my time living there.

New friendships were gradually formed and work was found – editing and writing for an aristocratic Thai lady, and teaching conversational English to University students. The editing and writing paid my rent and bills, teaching two evenings a week gave pocket money for coffees, street food and new released UK music and US movies on CD and DVD - all for a dollar each.

There was however another job I stumbled on.

Having my usual coffee at 5pm at the night market's Starbucks I listen to the conversation between two English women on the table next to mine.

"Yes," the one woman told the other. "They said they were looking for actors for a movie being made in Chiang Mai. They said to be at the hotel lobby at 6pm."

I knew the hotel they talked of. I looked to my watch. It was 5.15pm. Jumping on my scooter I dashed home, showered, put on my best shirt and jeans and raced to the hotel lobby spoken of. Arriving just before 6pm I stood with ten other westerners. A petite Thai woman with a clipboard approached us all.

"When I call your name, please stand over here," she pointed across the lobby. Each person did as told on hearing their name until only I remained.

"What is your name?" The woman with the clipboard asked.

I told her.

"But you are not on the list."

"I should be," I bluffed.

"Ok," she smiled and added me to the list. It was easy as that.

The movie was called Vampires: The Turning. I was in two scenes, one in a market place, the other on an airplane set.

Through this I got to know the Thai casting director. Telling me they had difficulty finding westerners I asked him if he would like me to find them for him when a movie came about. He agreed. Now I had first call to all further productions.

Even though there was an awful lot of waiting around, my all but brief appearances on the silver screen were good fun, and the food provided was also good – imported English bacon on one occasion.

I was in a Thai Charlie's Angles, the British comedy-drama Auf Wiedersehen Pet, Stealth, another Thai movie set in a nightclub (where I sat at a bar with an American friend and drank the beers given to us throughout the shoot), and a part in one of Thailand's soap operas. Set in a hotel I was cast as a foreign tourist walking past reception carrying two large suitcases.

In my six month sabbatical from Chiang Mai I had found myself on a film set in Chicago. For a millisecond I can just be seen watching Nicolas Cage ice skating in the film 'The Weatherman'.

Ten years in the future I would play a foreign tourist once again in a Nepalese Telecom commercial (it can be found on YouTube). For an eight hour shoot I was paid a curry lunch and a can of coke.

Still visiting Wat Chedi Luan most evenings I now carried a camera with me. One photograph taken of several black Buddhas standing in a line inside the temple found its way onto the BBC News website, as did several other images taken around Chiang Mai.

A journalist saw my portfolio and a job was offered taking photos for the city's magazine. I accepted.

My first job was photographing an annual three day Thai boxing event on the Thai/Burmese border where Thai's fought Burmese to dispel any animosities gathered over the previous year. Standing ringside on the ropes I photographed some of the one hundred three minute fights during each day, and gained my first front cover - a Burmese boxer's hemp bound fists clenched together at his waist.

While covering the boxing contacts were made for The Karen National Liberation Army, their camp laying just a few miles into Myanmar from where we stood beside battered and bruised boxers.

Another story was covered at a local snake farm and I got my second front cover photo. This time it was of a snake charmer kissing a black cobra's hooded head.

Laying down to take the photo my camera's click caught the cobra's attention. It swung round to me with a hiss. Lowering my camera I realised I had misjudged my camera lens' focal length. The snake was only three feet from my nose. I backed away, carefully.

With new ventures presenting themselves in ways of movies, liberation armies, boxers and hooded cobras, wanderlust pulled on me again.

I resisted its call, at my peril.

I have learnt over years of travel that when it's time to move on, it's time to move on. The life I had made for myself on my second stay in Chiang Mai was full and rich. I pushed wanderlust's call away. Within a week my life in the city I had come to know twice fell apart.

It is my belief/experience, that if you push against where you are supposed to be going, the universe, the powers that be, whatever you care to believe, will keep throwing situations of strife at you until you take the path you are supposed to walk. At last succumbing to these pushes it took five days to pack up my apartment, sell my scooter and say my goodbyes.

I left my Chiang Mai for England - where the universe continued its push on me. Three months later I stood on mainland China's soil.

A year after leaving Thailand and with a stay in China, I arrived in India. India was where I was supposed to be. The pushing stopped.

I have only returned to Chiang Mai once.

Four years after leaving the place I had called home I rode a scooter along Old City streets again.

I visited the house first rented with three others seven years earlier. New western tenets lived there now. I spent an afternoon sitting on the veranda of my old land lady's teak house. We were joined by her sister and we laughed together of how she would jump up and try to swipe my ear in the day's early hours.

I arrived at Wat Chedi Luan at 6pm on the first night of my return. On entering those red threadbare rugs were gone, as was a solitude once found. In place was a narrow strip of new red carpet running through the centre of the temple. Long gaudy paper lanterns hung from the rafters where bird's once roosted, obstructing the view of the tall golden Buddhas standing at the far end of the temple.

A visit to the Irish Bar which had seen many a good night confirmed time had passed. In a bar once filled with dancing and singing revelers, empty white clothed tables stood awaiting customers for their evening meal.

Only two people remained of the two sets of people met with over a period of three years. Although good to see them, Chiang Mai was not as it was. To me at least. I stayed for only two nights before returning to a Bangkok that in my eyes will never change.

I felt no sorrow in seeing how my old home had changed. Teachings learnt during my time skipping across Asia had taught me that nothing is permanent. That everything is ever changing.

This was brought home by the words of a fellow countryman.

'The past is a foreign country; they do things differently there.'

Chapter Thirty-Five

Everywhere

The Kindness of Strangers

Everywhere

To travel not knowing when a return home will be requires many elements - self-sufficiency and a curiosity of mind as well as an open one are just some. Yet there is one factor which is vital for a life on the road, no matter how long that period in your life may be. That factor is learning how to embrace solitude.

Friends you never imagined before arrive, some for a day, some for a week, a month or year, some even stay a life time no matter what distance separates you, but embracing solitude is key. An aloneness not loneliness in time spent alone.

For how else can you expect the mind and soul to progress when not confronting personnel pasts and those existential thoughts which at times writhe within us?

Even when finding myself in a group of other travellers exploring new places together a craving for aloneness came - and once met with so embraced. A recharging of self, ready to be within the company of others once more.

A first visit to Nepal saw to my first stretch of solitude.

Besides Pokhara's teardrop shaped Phewa Lake, I spent two months with only occasional moments of small talk with others.

Leaving Thailand and the comfort of others it took the first of those two months to acclimatise - only then did I fall into solitude's embrace. After those two months a metaphorical veil was lifted. I saw and understood that there is more to the world we know. That there is a better way to act and so be.

An anomaly occurs when at peace in solitude. A realisation comes that in order to truly grow the company of others is as much a necessity as time spent in solitary contentment. Life then consists of a constant flit between solitude and the company of others. This soon becomes a way of life for the lone traveller.

It is often when in the company of another that something you cannot search for, buy or hold arrives to you. Kindness.

It started with a chocolate. This was when I first recognised kindness can be found within the utmost simplicity of actions.

Walking over actors names held within pink five pointed stars, Los Angeles' Hollywood Boulevard seemed a million miles from The Cook Islands. Arriving that morning from the South Pacific, the friend I had flown to LA with had a flight back to the UK that evening. For now we forgot about an impending farewell and enjoyed the sights. My friend darted into a shop. I waited outside.

Appearing with a smile they handed me a single chocolate wrapped in gold paper. I can't remember what it tasted like, nor could I tell you what the inscription said on its gilded paper. All I remember is the kindness surrounding that simple act of giving with no want in return.

This is just one example of kindness met with on my travels. Two examples concern Coca-Cola. The first in Mexico when a fellow bus traveller saw my concern on leaving our bus and standing before gun totting black uniformed soldiers. The second in Kathmandu, an hour or so after Nepal's earthquake of May 2015 struck, where in the hotel I would come to call home for the next few years I was given an ice cold bottle of coke - once again to settle the nerves.

In my early years in Thailand, a Bangkok local took me on a ferry ride on the capital's Menem River to visit Koh Kret island, famous for its traditional Mon-style pottery of terracotta bowls and vases.

Each time I went to pay they would shake their head not allowing me to do so, even though they had little themselves.

In George Town, Malaysia, the owner of the hotel I stayed in took me to a Buddhist temple famed in Malaysia for its fortune telling abilities. This was followed by a lunch sampling Penang's street food in places unknown to foreign visitors.

So too did I encounter such kindness in another hotel. This time in Siem Reap, Cambodia in 2019.

As early evening came said hotel manager pulled up in the hotel courtyard on his motor bike.

"Come," he said. "We visit Angkor Wat."

Riding into dusk we circled the 12th century complex of hundreds of temple and shrine. A holy setting built to provide a spiritual home for the Hindu god Vishnu, before becoming a Buddhist temple.

As darkness fell we stopped at a small roadside restaurant. The hotel receptionist waited for us there, as did a feast of roasted chicken and Cambodian dishes await us all.

The list of kindness' shown to this lonesome traveller is more than can be counted. On each occasion, encountering the kindness of others I have been humbled by such acts, and at times a world weary traveller has had his faith restored in human nature.

His Holiness the 14th Dalai Lama once said:

"Be kind whenever possible. It is always possible"

It *is* always possible to show kindness to others.

As kindness to another brings happiness to its recipient, so too does it bring happiness to its provider.

This is the secret to harbouring inner happiness within ourselves.

By making others happy through kindness and compassion, so too does happiness arrive to its bearer. It's as simple as that.

For centuries philosophers of the world have searched to find the recipe for happiness in life. It purely comes down to this: To find happiness, all you have to do is make another happy.

Of all my travels across the world as well as across the decades, it is not so much the views, sunsets, temples and cityscapes I remember most. It is the acts of kindness once shown to a stranger in a foreign land.

The End

Also By The Author

Fiction

Subway of Light

Sometimes a second chance is all we need

A novel by
Julian Bound

No one can tread your path but you, yet we should never dismiss those who join us on our journey from time to time.

Following an accident, Josh finds himself sat alone at the back of an empty New York subway car on a deserted station, his memory gone and with no recollection of how he arrived there.

A man approaches and introduces himself as George. George tells Josh he has been taken out of his life to partake on a journey on the train. Acting as a guide, George explains their train will make several stops and that each station they visit may begin to seem familiar to him. Arriving at their first stop, Josh and George witness a young couple meet for the first time. George tells Josh that the young couple are soul mates rediscovering one another again.

The ensuing stations Josh and George's subway train stops at follows the young couple's life through the years as they experience courtship, marriage, tragedy and happiness. In watching their lives unfold, Josh gradually begins to gain awareness through George's guidance, until, as his memory starts to return, it is Josh himself who must decide the fate of his own final destination.

'*Subway of Light*' is a healing book of love found, lost, and regained through the act of belief and trust, not only within ourselves but in others.

The story of one man's awakening

By Way Of The Sea

One Monk's Journey of Discovery

A novel by
Julian Bound

Struggling with his beliefs a Tibetan Buddhist monk begins a journey to see the sea he has always dreamt of. Travelling on foot through Tibet, Nepal and India to reach his goal, those he encounters along the way start to restore a faith lost to him.

After visiting Namsto Lake as a young novice, Tenzin has longed to stand before seas never witnessed in a landlocked Tibet. Coming of age he leaves Lhasa's Gyuto Monastery and travels southwards on his quest. Travelling through his homelands he walks beside holy lakes and over high attitude mountain passes until reaching Nepal's border.

Continuing south to Kathmandu and to Pokhara's sacred lake he arrives to the town of Lumbini on Nepal's border with India. There within the gardens of Buddha's birthplace Tenzin's fading beliefs begin to be rekindled.

Crossing into India he journeys south once more and soon meets with a path he is destined to take.

Encountering many on his travels each hold a valuable lesson for Tenzin as together they explore the concepts of attachment, impermanence, kindness and compassion and karma and reincarnation. With each insight gained he continues onwards, his pursuit to see the sea accompanied by a want to understand the faith in which he has been raised.

The Geisha And The Monk

*Two souls born thousands of miles apart
each shall follow a similar path*

A novel
Julian Bound

KYOTO, JAPAN 1876

A girl is born into a lineage of famous geishas. Following her upbringing and training within a Tokyo geisha house her true identity is at last revealed.

GYANTSE, TIBET 1876

A boy is born into a small farming community. Recognised to be the reincarnation of a revered Lama he is taken to Shigatse's Tashi Lhunpo Monastery, it is there his unique destiny is unveiled.

SAN FRANCISCO, USA 1900

At the dawning of a new century fate brings them together, a lifetime away from all they have ever known.

With their stories running in parallel, *'The Geisha and The Monk'* tells of the training of a Tokyo geisha and a Tibetan Buddhist monk. Although coming from different backgrounds both share a matching destiny, one discovered when meeting on the shores of San Francisco's harbour front.

'Eventually, two souls destined to meet shall do so, their connection instantly recognised within the eyes of the other.'

LIFE'S HEART ETERNAL

One Man's Journey Through The Centuries

A novel by
Julian Bound

'My name is Franc Barbour. I was born on the 20th July 1845 in the town of Saumur, deep in the heart of the Loire Valley, France. The truth of the matter is I simply never died.'
These are the opening words a young nurse reads in an old leather bound journal given to her by a stranger. She soon uncovers the story of one man's journey through the centuries.

Following Franc's path from 1845 until present day, 'Life's Heart Eternal' is a tale of how our actions in each lifetime often hold consequences in the next.

With Franc's travels across the world in his endless years, the reader anticipates his next encounter with those reincarnated from his past and of what lessons each shall meet with.

'For who has never wondered what it would be like to live forever?'

The Soul Within

*Because everyone longs for
their soul to be touched*

A novel
Julian Bound

*In releasing our thoughts towards a lifetime imagined,
only then may we have the life our soul awaits.*

Falling ill in his home town of Puri on India's eastern coastline, a boy is visited by his spirit guide. Taking him on a journey around a tranquil lake, together they observe those living along its banks.

As his guide explains the life lessons they encounter through her subtle teachings, the boy's emerging awareness to matters of the soul leads him to discover the reasons behind their meeting as his story unfolds.

A heart-warming tale of awareness, 'The Soul Within' offers its readers an insight into another's awakening, guided by the love and kindness held within us all.

OF FUTURES PAST

A story of past lives and reincarnation.

A novel
Julian Bound

Following her death, a young New York art restorer finds herself on a beach accompanied by George, her spirit guide.

Explaining she now resides between lives George guides her to a cliff top library. Inside she finds a book containing all the past lives she has ever lived. Seated together they read her past lifetimes lived throughout the centuries.

Be it an artist's model of 16th century Renaissance Italy, a geisha of ancient Japan, or a Tibetan Buddhist monk living in the foothills of the Himalayas, each lifetime holds answers towards the progression of the soul, as seen in those met with through the years, be them friend or foe, or ultimately the soul mate she encounters in her many lifetimes.

Between uncovering the events of her previous lives, George explains the reasons for the situations that unfolded within her past, his explanations bringing forward an awareness of the characteristics unique to her own soul and of the trials she at times has been faced with.

Of Futures Past is a story of discovery, offering an insight into how our actions in one lifetime can effect moments in those to follow, shown with subtle teachings of love and compassion.

NON-FICTION

IN THE FIELD

A Memoir by Julian Bound

From National Geographic photographic contributor and award winning documentary photographer Julian Bound, tales of capturing world events, conflicts and culture on camera whilst living on the road as a documentary photographer.

From the child soldiers of a Burmese liberation army to photographing the moment Nepal's 2015 earthquake struck, *In The Field* tells of encounters within Java's active volcanoes, Cairo's Arab Spring, Bangkok's coup d'état, and a venture into covert photography for a government in exile.

Alongside tales of conflict and natural disasters another journey is recounted, one which saw to documenting Buddhism throughout Asia and South East Asia, including Bhutan's fortress monasteries, Tibet's remote temples, chanting Tantric monks of the Himalayas, and meeting His Holiness the 14th Dalai Lama at his 80th birthday celebrations.

Stories Featured Include:

The Karen National Liberation Army
Nepal's Maoist Civil War
Rebellion on the streets of Bangkok
Tibetan refugees
A journey through Tibet
Mumbai's Dharavi slums
Cambodia's Killing Fields
The Nepal earthquakes of 2015
His Holiness the 14th Dalai Lama

An account of life on the road as a documentary photographer.

Non-Fiction

The Seven Deadly Sins And The Seven Heavenly Virtues

As viewed in religion, ancient mythology and art and literature

by Julian Bound

The Seven Deadly Sins and the antidotes of the Seven Heavenly Virtues have been depicted throughout history in forms of both Greek and Roman mythology and in the world of art and literature.

Perceived as being associated within the doctrine of the Christian faith, the eastern religions of Buddhism, Hinduism and Sikhism all share a parallel view of the seven sins and virtues, yet are expressed in the theology of different precepts.

'The Seven Deadly Sins and The Seven Heavenly Virtues' examines the similarities of each sin and virtue within religions of the world, and of the portrayal in mythology and art and literature.

'The Seven Deadly Sins and The Seven Heavenly Virtues' also invites the reader to identify which sin they are prone to and of what virtue best displays their greatest qualities; the result of which is an exploration of the self within the aspects of the seven sins and seven virtues, and so acting as a guide for each soul's unique individual path.

PHOTOGRAPHY BOOKS

THE MIDDLE WAY

Photography and Words
by
Julian Bound

A 6,331mile/10,156km photographic journey through seven Buddhist countries in seven months. Documenting the life, traditions and culture of Buddhism in India, Nepal, Bhutan, Tibet, Myanmar, Thailand and Cambodia.

From McLeod Ganj, India's 'Little Lhasa', to a gathering of 5,000 Buddhist monks and nuns in Lumbini, Nepal, birth place of Buddha, then onwards through the secluded Kingdom of Bhutan, the high altitudes of Tibet's remote monasteries, the golden temples of Myanmar and Thailand and the riverside shrines of Cambodia.

Travelling through altitudes of 16,900 feet /5,150 metres to sea level, and between temperatures ranging from -18 to 38 degrees, a journey of discovery on the path of the middle way.

Photography Books

Portraits of Nepal

Photography and Words
by
Julian Bound

Kathmandu
Sindhupalchowk
Pokhara

Portraits from Nepal's capital Kathmandu, the village of Chhaimale, the Northern district of Sindhupalchowk on the Tibetan borderlands and the lakeside city of Pokhara.

A collection of unique portraiture of the Nepalese people taken over a four year period. Depicting Nepalese life and culture in colour and black and white photographs.

About The Author

Born in England, Julian is a documentary photographer, film maker and author. With photographic work featured on the BBC news, his photographs have been published in National Geographic, New Scientist and the international press. His work focuses on the social documentary of world culture, religion and traditions, with time spent studying meditation with the Buddhist monks of Tibet and Northern Thailand and spiritual teachers of India's Himalaya region.

His photography work includes documenting the child soldiers of Myanmar's Karen National Liberation Army, the Arab Spring of 2011, Cairo, Egypt, and Thailand's political uprisings of 2009 and 2014 in Bangkok.

With portraiture of His Holiness the 14th Dalai Lama, Julian has extensively photographed the Tibetan refugees of Nepal and India. His other projects include the road working gypsies of Rajasthan, India, the Dharavi slums of Mumbai, the riverside squatter slums of Yogyakarta and the sulphur miners at work in the active volcanoes of Eastern Java, Indonesia.

Present for the Nepal earthquakes of 2015 he documented the disaster whilst working as an emergency deployment photographer for various NGO and international embassies in conjunction with the United Nations and the World Wildlife Foundation.

With numerous published photography books Julian is also the author of novels of *Subway of Light*, *The Geisha and The Monk*, *By Way of The Sea* and *Life's Heart Eternal*.

When not on the road in Asia, Julian is based in the UK.

Some chapters in this book include excerpts taken from:

In The Field
Memoirs of life on the road as a documentary photographer.
by Julian Bound

Available paperback and Ebook

Printed in Great Britain
by Amazon